TAMWORTH
PAST AND PRESENT

TAMWORTH
PAST AND PRESENT

IN ASSOCIATION WITH THE

JOHN HARPER

First published in Great Britain in 2002 by
The Breedon Books Publishing Company Limited
Breedon House, 3 The Parker Centre,
Derby, DE21 4SZ.

Paperback edition published in Great Britain in 2012 by The Derby Books Publishing
Company Limited, 3 The Parker Centre, Derby, DE21 4SZ.

ISBN 978-1-78091-174-8

CONTENTS

Acknowledgements … … … … … … … … … … … … … …6

Introduction … … … … … … … … … … … … … … …7

Upper Gungate … … … … … … … … … … … … … …8

Bell Corner … … … … … … … … … … … … … … …19

Hospital Street … … … … … … … … … … … … … …21

Lower Gungate … … … … … … … … … … … … …25

Colehill … … … … … … … … … … … … … … …41

Bolebridge Street … … … … … … … … … … … …45

Victoria Road … … … … … … … … … … … … …58

Tamworth Station … … … … … … … … … … … …63

Albert Road … … … … … … … … … … … … … …70

Marmion Street … … … … … … … … … … … … …74

Spinning School Lane … … … … … … … … … … …76

Church Lane … … … … … … … … … … … … … …78

Corporation Street … … … … … … … … … … … …83

Aldergate … … … … … … … … … … … … … … …88

Silver Street … … … … … … … … … … … … … …96

The Holloway and Ladybank … … … … … … … …102

Lady Bridge … … … … … … … … … … … … … …107

The Castle Grounds … … … … … … … … … … …110

Market Street … … … … … … … … … … … … …119

George Street … … … … … … … … … … … … …137

Church Street … … … … … … … … … … … … …162

Lichfield Street … … … … … … … … … … … … …195

ACKNOWLEDGEMENTS

I am indebted to the following people who have kindly loaned photographs for this book.
Christine Wood; Frank Caldwell of Tamworth Castle Museum; Richard Hughes of Tamworth
Co-operative Society Ltd; Roger Pointon; Bill Sheppard; Chris Gibson; Rod Farrant; Guy Smith; Mary
Edwards; Winnie Claridge; Mary James; John Latham; Arthur Higginson; Phyllis Higginson; Peter Gould;
Jean Edwards; Douglas Thompson; Brian Hawkins; Gerry Day; and many unknown photographers whose
work appears within these pages. This project would not have been possible, however, without prolific
Tamworth Herald photographers Paul Barber and John Walker, and their predecessor, the late Tom Harris.
Their brilliant work over many years has contributed so much to the town's photographic archives.
Thanks also to Emerson Todd, whose technical expertise in scanning some pictures has been invaluable. I
also wish to acknowledge a debt of thanks to Tamworth Herald columnist Mabel Swift, former Tamworth
Herald employee Jack Longsorth, whose research on Tamworth Castle Bowls Club was invaluable, and
Tamworth Castle's former assistant curator Richard Sulima, whose research has contributed inestimable
information about old Tamworth.
When compiling the text, the published works of Charles Ferrers Palmer, H.C. Mitchell, Tony Aldous and
Henry Wood have been hugely helpful, as have the writings of county archeologist Bob Meeson, Tamworth
historian Peter Edden, Nigel Morris and the Revd David Juliano.
I also wish to record my appreciation to Tamworth Herald editor Sam Holliday and deputy editor Phil
Shanahan for their encouragement.
Finally, I am indebted to my dear wife, Maureen, without whose belief and unstinting support I would
never have completed this project.

DEDICATION

THIS BOOK IS DEDICATED TO THE PEOPLE OF TAMWORTH, IN HOPEFUL ANTICIPATION THAT THE TOWN OF THE FUTURE WILL NEVER LOSE SIGHT OF ITS PRECIOUS PAST.

Over 250 of the 650 pictures published in this book were taken by photographer Paul Barber, including many archive shots from the 1960s and 70s and all of the modern photographs.

Born in Victoria Road, Tamworth, Paul Barber lived in Wigginton
until he was four years old, when his family moved to the then new
Gillway estate. He started taking photographs at the age of 11 using
a plastic camera from Woolworth's. He continued taking photographs
throughout his youth at Flax Hill Primary and Mercian Boys' schools.
Upon leaving school in the late 1960s, Paul was taken on by
Tamworth photographer Garfield Snow and went on to run his own
studio in Colehill, during which time he began working on a freelance
basis for the Tamworth Herald, joining the staff full time in 1997.
'It was around 1967 when I noticed that the town I had grown up in
was changing dramatically, with demolition everywhere and new
building going up,' Paul says. 'I decided to record these changes with
my camera.
'Perhaps my biggest regret is the loss of old Church Street, which has
been completely ruined. If only the shop frontages had been retained
and restored with new development hidden behind – what a beautiful
street it would have been today.'
Paul is married to Jenny. They have both lived in Tamworth all their
lives.

6

INTRODUCTION

WE are all walking through history – but Tamworth is history. The town has existed for at least 1,400 years and will be here long after present generations have departed this life. The decisions we make, however, will have a crucial effect on the town that our successors inherit.

As early as the eighth century Tamworth was an Anglo Saxon royal borough in which the kings of Mercia resided.

Precious little of the building fabric of the time has made it down the centuries, but we do have our great landmark buildings – the Parish Church, the Castle and the Town Hall. We also have the streets, which even today wind along ancient routes trodden by Tamworthians of the past who felt as passionately about their town as anyone today.

The town centre that existed 50 years ago would have been familiar to many born in preceding eras. It had evolved over the centuries, with each generation adding their own buildings and putting new uses to older ones. Change came slowly and, on the whole, brought significant improvements.

The Tamworth that existed in 1952 possessed a rich architectural legacy which, were it intact today, would have enormous tourist potential.

By the 1960s, however, this gentle evolution had turned into revolution with 'growth' and 'expansion' the buzzwords of the day. Demolition sites sprung up on every street, and centuries-old masonry was replaced by modern concrete and glass in an orgy of destruction that still makes many older Tamworthians seethe with rage.

Huge housing estates, new shopping centres, leisure facilities and roads were created to serve the expanding town, which has provided homes and employment for countless new townsfolk.

In another 50 years, perhaps, the 1960s architecture that is today so despised by many may well be looked upon with fondness by those who grew up with it. It is an attempt to bridge this gap between the old Tamworth and the new that this book is intended.

Some of the earliest views are by Etienne Bruno Hamel, a talented artist who also possessed great business acumen. He started a tape-making factory in the town which flourished right up until 1980.

Hamel's 1829 Illustrations of Tamworth give us a fascinating, but perhaps slightly rose-coloured glimpse of how the town centre looked in the reign of George IV.

The advent of photography, however, allows us a more realistic view of how the town appeared in bygone years. Wartime restrictions and post-war austerity in the 1940s and 50s resulted in far fewer photographs being taken. This has deprived us of

seeing the town's streets at their best because by the 1960s – when many pictures in this book were taken – scores of old buildings had fallen into serious dilapidation and were awaiting demolition. But thanks to likes of Tamworth Photographic Club, who recorded many threatened street scenes, and particularly Paul Barber, who took it upon himself to photograph old buildings before they vanished for ever, we have a comprehensive record of the last days of old Tamworth.

Enormous changes have taken place over the last 50 years. Whether they have been for the better or worse depends on your individual viewpoint. The comments made throughout the ensuing pages are my own and should not be taken as definitive.

This book does not profess to be a history of Tamworth, merely a photographic tour of how the serried streets of yesteryear were transformed into the bustling town centre of today.

It has been impossible to include every street and every building, but I hope the photographs and illustrations contained herein will encourage readers to take a deeper interest in the buildings that make up the town centre, and be sufficient to take you on a leisurely stroll through Tamworth past and present.

John Harper,
February 2002.

UPPER GUNGATE

Right: Our tour of Tamworth begins at the northern approach to the town centre. This grand Victorian villa stood on the crest of Upper Gungate hill, just off the Comberford Road. Known as Hillcrest, it was owned by the Thornburn family who for many years ran Tamworth's two picture houses, the Grand and the Palace cinemas. In 1961, the house was sold to a firm of property developers for £3,500 and was allowed to become derelict.

Left: Goshen, a large imposing house standing near to Hillcrest, was the former home of Tamworth Town Clerk John Matthews, until his death in 1919, when it was acquired by Miss Shaw. As was the case with Hillcrest, this outstanding residence was bought by property developers who proceeded to demolish both houses in readiness for a new residential estate.

Below: In 1966–7 an intimate 46-home development, subsequently known as Hillcrest Close, was built on the site of the two fine houses pictured above and left.

Left: Here we see construction of Hillcrest Close in January 1967. The grounds in which the original Hillcrest house stood covered more than an acre and boasted over 100 trees.

Above: Hillcrest Close today, photographed from the same spot as above. All that remains of the old houses are fragments of roof tile and brick that occasionally turn up in the gardens of homes now occupying the site. Although demolition of such fine houses as Hillcrest and Goshen is regrettable, this small scale, private development has proved a great success, and could have been repeated more often on other sites around the town.

Above: Upon leaving Comberford Road and entering Upper Gungate we arrive at the former Queen Elizabeth Grammar School, which was established on this site in 1867 following demolition of the previous school building in Lower Gungate. In 1979 the school was amalgamated with the Mercian and Perrycrofts schools as a 1,220 place comprehensive.

Below: This 1935 photograph shows the grammar school cricket team (front row) and the old boys' team (rear) with the 1867 buildings behind them. These were largely rebuilt in 1937. In the centre is headmaster Mr F. Burkitt and Mr E.S. Warrilow. The school is now part of Queen Elizabeth's Mercian School.

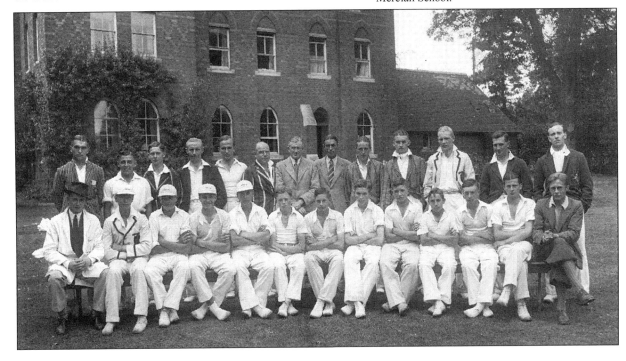

Above: The Fountain Junction was so named after a Victorian drinking fountain built in 1898 on a triangular piece of land known locally as The Hand, between the Comberford Road, left, and Ashby Road, right.

Above: Viewed from the old grammar school entrance, this is how the Fountain Junction looked in the mid-1960s.

Right: The fountain was removed in 1968 to accommodate a new road junction, which is even today known as Fountain Junction. Worried locals, dismayed by the loss of such a well-known landmark, were assured that the monument would be reassembled at some other more suitable site in the town, possibly the Castle Grounds. Seen here in 2002, traffic signals and road signs are modern necessities, but poor substitutes for such a recognisable feature of the town.

Left: Standing opposite the former Queen Elizabeth Grammar School, the fountain was given to the town by Tamworth benefactor Mrs Hutton, in memory of her late husband. The Victorian curiosity was made of red Peterhead granite and boasted brass fittings and a lantern. It consisted of three separate drinking troughs, for horses, dogs and people, with the cups bearing the words, 'Tamworth Corporation', and the column inscribed with the Biblical quotation, 'I was thirsty and ye gave me drink'. In mediaeval times, the town gallows stood on the site. (Photo: William Burdett)

Above: Mrs Hutton, in her carriage, visiting the fountain. This is the only known picture of this generous lady who did so much for Tamworth.

Above: After being dismantled in 1968, the fountain was promptly 'lost' and for 30 years its whereabouts remained a mystery. Following a campaign by the Tamworth Herald, some broken fragments were unearthed in an overgrown corner of the local council's works depot at Kettlebrook. Further pieces were recovered from private gardens. Sadly, the column and lantern have never been found… although the search goes on.

Above: Thanks to the intervention of Tamworth Civic Society, the monument was pieced together and made into an attractive centrepiece at the MacGregor Tithe sheltered housing development in Hospital Street. Pictured at the unveiling in November 1999 are Civic Society president Joyce Smith and Arthur Taylor, past chairman of Waterloo Housing Association.

Above: There can be few more evocative views of old Tamworth than this 1829 lithographic print showing Upper Gungate, looking towards town. It is the work of Etienne Bruno Hamel, who has used a little 'artistic licence' in stretching Tamworth Castle's Norman tower to make it more prominent, and making the tower of St Editha's Church a little slimmer.

Above: This 1995 photograph of Upper Gungate is taken from exactly the same viewpoint as above. The Victorians and Edwardians lined the embankments with stone and built splendid homes and villas on either side. Amazingly, the tall copper beech tree has survived from the 1829 picture and today stands in the grounds of the former Mayfield Home for the Elderly, on the corner with Croft Street.

Above: The Mount public house had originally been built as a private house, but was found structurally suitable for conversion into licensed premises when it came up for sale in 1958. It was opened by the Mayor of Tamworth, Councillor K.A. Muggleston, in April 1959 and served as a Mitchells and Butlers inn for around 25 years.

Above: A 1999 aerial view of Upper Gungate taken from the tower of Tamworth Church.

Above: In 1989, the Mount pub was demolished and consulting rooms built on the site for the Aldergate Medical Practice. The view is from Croft Street.

Above: Despite some slightly eccentric features, the medical centre's design pays due architectural homage to the Victorian and Edwardian villas that extend up to the Fountain Junction and beyond. The surgery opened in January 1990.

Above: Photographed just before demolition in the 1960s, this row of 19th-century workers' houses stood adjacent to the Mount pub's main entrance.

Above: Known locally as the Dog Cottages, the houses were situated on Upper Gungate's western stretch and had originally been part of a larger row extending down to Salters Lane. They acquired their name from a public house that originally stood on the vacant plot on the extreme left of this mid-1960s view.

Above: The same view today, as pictured left, showing modern homes built back from the original building line to allow for such modern fancies as front gardens. In the distance, the town's skyline has taken on a new shape.

Left: In its last days the Dog Inn was kept by landlord Albert Faulkner, one of three brothers who each ran a separate pub. The tiny premises were deemed unsuitable for modernisation, however, and so the licence was transferred to a nearby property which became the Mount. When closed in 1958, the licensing chairman described the Dog as the 'last call' for professional men living in Wigginton and Ashby roads. Pictured here in the 1920s, the gentlemen standing in the doorway are: Left to right, licensee Joseph Henry Salt (Senior), funeral director E.J. Cole, and Henry Salt (Junior).

Above: A 1970s view looking towards the Tamworth Co-operative Society's funeral parlour. The Co-op took over the undertaking business from the family of the late E.J. Cole in 1950.

Right: The same view as above in 2002. A pleasant, small scale housing development, Oldbury Court, was sandwiched between the funeral parlour and the railway line in the 1990s.

Left: This centuries-old row of shops and cottages had echoed to the sounds of stagecoaches clattering their busy way into and out of the town centre past an ancient milestone (below) which was repositioned against the Health Centre's perimeter wall (below left).

Right: Looking towards the town centre, the familiar buildings lining Upper Gungate's approach to Bell Corner were pulled down in 1981 to make way for extensions to Tamworth Health Centre.

Above: On 3 April 1967, photographer Paul Barber recorded the demolition of cottages facing the forecourt of the Marmion Motors garage.

Left: The last remnants of the cottages are cleared away by demolition men who were frequent visitors to Tamworth throughout the 1960s and '70s.

Right: Pictured here soon after opening in November 1968, few would disagree that the modern Tamworth Health Centre is a building of mind-numbing banality...even by the slipshod standards of the 1960s.

Below: Today the woeful architecture is partially hidden away behind a perimeter wall. Perhaps the wall should have been built several feet higher!

Above: Standing opposite the Lower Gungate shops and cottages was Marmion Motors garage, pictured here in 1970s. The business was established on this site in the 1930s by brothers George and James Rose. On the horizon is Tamworth College of Further Education, which opened in 1953.

Above: By 1990, not only the price of petrol had gone up. A large canopy now covered the garage forecourt.

Above: Road chaos at the Bell Corner junction following a fall of snow on 8 December 1990. The picture was taken at 10am.

Above: The premises of James Eadie, brewers, wine and spirit merchants of Burton upon Trent, stood on the corner of Upper Gungate and Albert Road, c.1895-1900. The large house became Agnes Kendrick's fashionable hairdressing shop which, together with a small row of cottages in Upper Gungate and Jeffcoate's carpentry yard, were demolished to make way for Rose Brothers' Marmion Motors garage.

Left: The view in 2002, pictured from the same spot as above.

Above: Demolition of the renamed Marmion Ford garage in September 1993.

Bell Corner

Above: One of Tamworth's most famous landmarks, the picturesque Old Bell Inn dripped with all the period charm and character of a bygone age. When the centuries-old coaching inn closed on 23 June 1959, the first pint was poured at the town's newest public house, the Riftswood on Comberford Road, where the Bell licence had been transferred. The ancient hostelry was simply boarded-up and left to the elements before being demolished in 1966 to make way for a traffic island that never materialised.

Above: The view from the same spot as above in 2002. The loss of such a unique building as the Bell is incalculable. The old pub had provided a hugely impressive entrance to the town centre, whereas the present view leaves much to be desired. It is testament to the affection in which it was held by Tamworth people that the area is still known as Bell Corner.

Above: Situated on a triangular piece of land between Aldergate and Hospital Street, Sheppard's Yard was established in 1723 by master horseman Jacob Sheppard. The stable buildings stood on Bell Corner for over 200 years, remaining in the same family throughout that time. The yard's reputation for 'breaking in' horses was so respected that even wild mustangs from as far away as America were sent here. It was said that the wildest horse could be ridden using nothing more than cotton for reins after it had been to Sheppard's. Among customers who sent horses here were a whole list of titled owners including Queen Victoria and King Edward VIII. The last horse of note to be kept at the yard was Colonel Harry Llewellyn's famous showjumper Foxhunter, star of two Olympic Games, winning bronze in London in 1948 and a team gold in Helsinki in 1952. The stables were pulled down in 1966 as part of the same aborted traffic scheme that claimed the Bell Inn. (Painting by Jean Snow)

Above: A 1970s view from the 'turret' of the former Rose Brothers' garage (see page 25) showing the site of what was Sheppard's Yard, now a car park. The town's General Hospital in the background has been replaced by a sheltered housing development known as MacGregor Tithe.

HOSPITAL STREET

Above: Looking from Aldergate across what was Sheppard's Yard, this row of Victorian terraced houses, known as Stranraer Place, stood in Hospital Street, near the Bell Corner junction with Lower Gungate. On the corner opposite the hospital was a tiny off-licence run by the Pickering family.

Right: A bulldozer flattens the homes to make way for the new Tamworth Health Centre. Kirkcowan Terrace, which stood behind these houses, was similarly dispatched.

Below: Photographer Paul Barber visited the scene in 1967, capturing the last moments for posterity.

Above: Demolition workers go about their business on the former Sheppard's Yard. The date is 8 February 1967. The section of hospital building in the background was known as the Hutton Wing, having been donated by the same benefactor who gave the town its famous Fountain drinking trough in Upper Gungate.

Above: Ten years later, Stranraer Place had become the Health Centre car park, while the perimeter of Sheppard's Yard was marked by up-ended kerbstones. The northern entrance to the town centre had never looked so shabby.

Above: G. & R. Watson's newsagent's shop (pictured in 1967) was a regular stopping off point for many travellers on their way to and from work. Built in 1862, Lockryan Place was comprised of the shop and two adjacent houses.

Left and Above: Watson's shop may have survived the 1967 blitz, but the reprieve was temporary. Demolition men returned in 1980 to finish the job. The crashing masonry was brilliantly captured by Paul Barber, whose camera had recorded many such scenes which by this time had become all too familiar.

Right: A modern view showing the same view as above. The redesigned road layout opened up the Hospital Street approach to Bell Corner, rendering the scene hardly recognisable.

Left: Tamworth's General Hospital (pictured in the 1930s) grew out of a small cottage hospital financed by the town's great benefactor, Revd William MacGregor. Opened on 1 January 1880, MacGregor's section is in the centre. The Hutton Wing was added in 1889 while the grand Memorial Hall and Porte-Cochere were opened by HRH the Duke of York, later King George VI, on 29 May 1924.

Right: The Miners' Welfare Fund contributed greatly to the development of the hospital, and when accommodation for nurses was required they once again came to the rescue, raising £2,807 for the building of a nurses' home (seen on the right of this 1996 picture) which was officially opened on 15 October 1930.

Left: The nurses' home and rear hospital buildings were demolished in 1997. Thankfully, the grand Memorial Hall, built to commemorate the 608 men from Tamworth and district who gave their lives in World War One, was saved along with the other original buildings fronting on to Hospital Street. The loss of the town centre hospital, however, caused much resentment among local people.

Right: With the building of a new hospital at Mile Oak (ungraciously named after Sir Robert Peel rather than Revd MacGregor, who founded the town's first hospital) what remained of the old buildings were incorporated into MacGregor Tithe, a fine sheltered housing development for the elderly which opened in 1998. The Memorial Hall, which had doubled as the hospital's waiting room, today serves as a quiet room in which residents can relax.

LOWER GUNGATE

Right: Turning back on ourselves, we return to Bell Corner where this 1966 Tamworth Herald news photograph gives a rare pre-demolition glimpse of buildings along Lower Gungate. The picture shows the scene shortly after demolition of the Bell Inn.

Below: Precious few of Tamworth's buildings have been designed with other than purely functional considerations in mind, but the former Rose Brothers' Central Garage is a welcome exception. George and James Rose, who secured the first Ford agency in Tamworth, displayed considerable enterprise in building such a prominent garage and house from which to run their business. The work was carried out in 1913 by local building contractor George Dent. This grainy photograph appeared in the Tamworth Herald in 1925.

Below: One of Tamworth's oldest streets, Lower Gungate was in 1289 recorded as Gumpiyat and in 1290 as Gumpigate. This view from Bell Corner on 18 January 1967 shows cables being laid along the western side. Demolition of the Bell Inn, which had stood in the right foreground, heralded an era of redevelopment that would spread along the street and into the town centre.

Above: This modern view from February 2002 shows the pleasant mix of 18th, 19th and 20th-century buildings standing opposite the former Rose's Garage (now Car Crazy) and Globe Inn. Many have been much altered and adapted over the years, but the row still retains a degree of old world charm that was once such a characteristic of Tamworth. Unfortunately, many of the shop fronts have been plastered with white paint – a regrettable modern trend that invariably spoils the general street scene.

Above: Pictured here in the 1960s, Gillam's newsagents stood opposite the Globe Inn. The extended shop stocked an impressive range of tobacco and confectionery products which, together with Airfix models and small toys, made it a popular stopping place for all ages.

Right: A modern view of the same shops showing how well the buildings were refurbished by Tamworth solicitor Peter Baxter, a passionate champion of quality architecture up until his death in 1991.

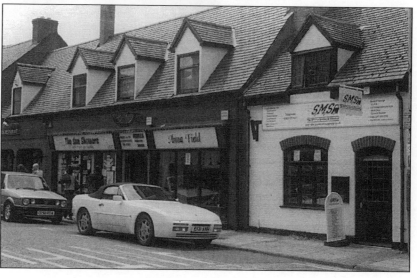

Above: Looking back from the junction with Church Lane, this 1960s view shows a new shop front being inserted into the Gillam's premises, which had previously been Whitehall's and later Everight Ltd.

Left: The same view as it appears today. In the 1970s, the two cottages on the junction with Church Lane, together with Smith's tobacconist store (later Sheldon Brothers' fruit and veg store), were replaced by a shop and office complex known as Bell Chambers. These incorporate the Gemini Cantonese restaurant.

Above: Hidden away at the rear of the buildings pictured above is Mitchell's Court, a modern development in the style of the 18th century built by Peter Baxter's widow, Janet, in the 1990s.

Above: Named after Henry Charles Mitchell, a respected Tamworth historian and stonemason who devoted much of his life to preserving the fabric of the town, the atmospheric architecture is delightful. The first shops opened in 1998.

Left: Moving back into Lower Gungate, we are confronted by more unwarranted demolition. The Star Inn had the appearance of a red brick house in a terraced row of houses that lined the eastern side of the street. This picture of demolition work underway was taken in 1970.

Left: Viewed from the same spot as above, a car park has replaced the old pub and houses.

Below: A rare view showing the Star Inn and houses that formerly stood between the Globe Inn and Rose's Garage.

Above: The dilapidated Globe Inn as it looked in 1992, and (below) in 1998, after the magnificent 1901 building had been returned to its Edwardian grandeur by local builder David Baxter.

Above: Photographed by Paul Barber shortly before demolition in 1968, these three-storey town houses stood opposite Church Lane. A fading advert for T. Watson, wholesale and retail newsagent of 4 Lochryan Place, is just visible on the side of the building nearest to us.

Left: Paul revisited the scene some days later, to discover that the bulldozers had not been idle.

Below: Looking from the same viewpoint today, the corner with Spinning School Lane is dominated by the former Palace Cinema (now the Palace Media Centre) and Embassy Leisure complex. Although of little architectural merit, these new buildings provided Tamworth with much needed recreational facilities.

Above: Prior to the arrival of what was hailed as 'leisure corner' the vacant site had been used as a make-shift car park, blighting the area for almost a decade.

Above: The new Palace Cinema was built by Tamworth Borough Council to replace the town's much lamented Palace Cinema in George Street, which closed in 1975. Perhaps a more appropriate title for the opening film should have been It Shouldn't Happen To A Cinema.

Cinema manager Mike Tooley threads the first film.

Above: The 325 seat picture house opened for Christmas of 1976, and closed as a cinema in 1991 when the town's new ten-screen UCI complex opened in Bolebridge. The building is now the Palace Media Centre.

Above: A long queue snakes around the under-construction Embassy Clipper Bar to see Batman II at the new Palace in 1989.

Above: Pictured by Paul Barber in March 1968 the former Ford and Rowley car component shop dated from around 1820. At the turn of the century, the buildings were Griffiths Engineers' Forge and Castle Cycle Works (below).

Above: The last picture as these familiar old Tamworth buildings bit the dust.

Right: The Embassy banqueting suite and associated bar was opened by Tamworth businessman Arthur Higginson in 1982. The facility, together with a bingo hall at the rear, provided a much needed boost to the town centre which up until that time boasted precious few entertainment venues of any size. The banqueting suite has subsequently been turned into a nightclub.

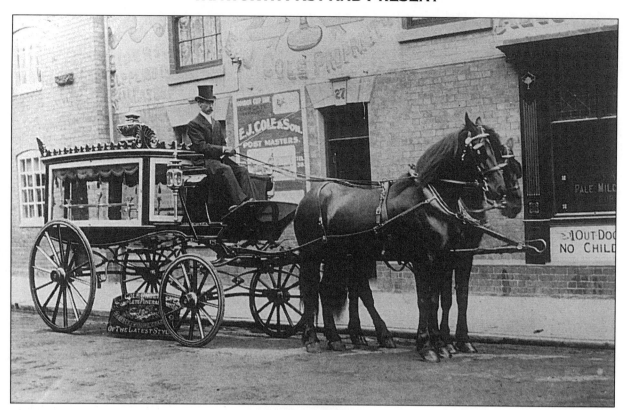

Above: Pictured in or around 1910, the gentleman at the reigns of the elegant glass hearse is Edward James Cole who, as well as being the town's undertaker, was also postmaster and proprietor of the Golden Cup public house, the frontage of which sported a painting of a huge golden goblet. Coming to Tamworth in 1880, Mr Cole was proprietor for 25 years. In the early days of his undertaking business (which operated from the rear of the pub), he was extremely proud of his fine team of black horses, although later adopted motor conveyances. In 1917, Mr Cole moved the funeral services to new premises which he had built in Upper Gungate (see page 15). Following Mr Cole's death in 1936, aged 76, the business was continued by his sons until 1950, when is was acquired by the Co-op.

Right, centre: In the 1930s, the premises were owned by butcher F. Sayce. By 1974, when this photograph was taken, the central portion had become Mercer's record and music shop, while the end section was occupied by butcher E. Jones.

Right, below: The Golden Cup emblem has long been painted over, and the old pub today – still with original woodwork surrounding the corner entrance – serves as a fish and chip shop.

Above: Queen Elizabeth's Free Grammar School, believed to have been founded by King Edgar in 963, was re-founded by Queen Elizabeth I in 1588. In 1678 it occupied this splendid brick schoolroom in Lower Gungate. Its demolition in 1867 – when a new grammar school was built on Ashby Road – caused such controversy that Sir Robert Peel, the third baronet, was moved to ask questions in Parliament. E.B. Hamel's 1829 engraving is the only view we have of this lost treasure of a building where Tamworth luminaries Thomas Guy and John Rawlet were taught.

Above: All was not lost, however, because incorporated in the block of four cottages built upon the stone foundation of the old school were decorative capitals which for over 200 years had adorned the façade of the 1668 building.

Above: Arched shop fronts were inserted in the 1970s, but the town's fleur-de-lys badge, together with three of the original five Ionic pilaster capitals, are still to be seen interspaced in brickwork between the first floor windows.

Right: Thomas Guy's original almshouses (pictured shortly before demolition in 1912) dated from 1678 when the great Tamworth benefactor had plans drawn up for a block of almshouses for seven poor women on the reputed site of the old mediaeval St George's Guildhall. Guy's mother was a native of Tamworth and he was educated at the town's grammar school, before later representing Tamworth in Parliament from 1695 to 1708.

Thomas Guy (1644–1724).

Above: The splendid almshouses we know today (seen here in the 1970s) may look as though they've stood for centuries, but they are relatively modern. Built in the free Georgian style, they date only from 1913. Faced with Woodville and Sandstock bricks with white Hollington stonework, they are a town centre delight.

Right: The almshouses (seen here in 2002) have been extended over the years, but the additions of 1928 and 1936 keenly reflect the 1913 design.

Above: Heavy traffic moving through Lower Gungate in 1990. The building with lowered blind is Miss Wylde's confectionery shop. The inside has been little altered since Victorian times with its period fireplace and red quarry tiles. The shop is one of Tamworth's timeless treasures.

Left: A modern view of the picture above. Pedestrianisation in 1994 vastly improved this section of the street – although the abundance of street furniture is unnecessary.

The former Prince of Wales public house was built in 1897 on the site of a previous pub, also called the Prince of Wales. Above the main entrance is a fine terracotta plaque which incorporates the monogram of William Godderidge Ashwood, the builder and first landlord, with the Prince of Wales' feathers. Pictured left in the 1960s and right as it looks today, attempts to attract a younger clientele have resulted in the pub being given its rather regrettable POW makeover.

Below: There were no more derelict buildings in Tamworth than these sadly neglected 15th-century cottages, pictured here in 1968. Together with neighbouring properties leading up to and along Little Church Lane, they are irrefutable proof that the hackneyed response of 'if we hadn't pulled them down they'd have fallen down' – so often used to excuse the demolition of old buildings – is just so much bunkum.

Above: The cottages were acquired by the Cooper brothers of Lullington who, together with builder Norman Phillips, set about bringing them back to life, ensuring that the centuries old beams – some nearly a foot thick – were preserved and the properties sympathetically restored. If other old buildings in the town had been treated in a similar manner Tamworth would not have been stripped of so much historic charm.

Above: Pictured here in 1990, before pedestrianisation, the restoration scheme gave us the most picturesque set of buildings in Tamworth. Hamlet's Wine Bar opened in 1976, and later became O'Neil's Irish bar. Today it is the Sir Robert Peel pub.

Above: Here we see Claridge's butchers and Wood's fish and poultry shops as they looked in the early 20th century. The bicycle is a Tamworth-made Porter Cycle, manufactured by William George Porter at his works in Bolebridge Street.

Above: An identical view in 2002. The author is standing in the same doorway as the gentleman in the picture above. New shop fronts have been inserted and the old store with the arched frontage has been rebuilt, today serving as Truckles cheese shop.

Right: The once attractive Dutch-style gable-ended property had fallen into an advanced state of dilapidation when this photograph was taken in the early 1960s. Standing next to Guy's almshouses, the arched doorway led to butcher Sidney Doggrell's slaughterhouse.

Below: In 1965, the former John English hairdressing shop (complete with a trendy façade) and associated Gungate Precinct development replaced the old buildings.

Above: The same view today as above. Bacons shoe shop now occupies premises formerly inhabited by Halfords, the bicycle and car accessory store.

Above: Although the first shops flung open their doors in August 1965, the Gungate Precinct wasn't officially opened until October 1966. But it hasn't aged well. The architecture, seen here in the 1970s, is a sedentary reminder of an era that saw the erection of countless bland, utilitarian shopping centres such as this that are today the blight of so many English towns and cities.

Left: Spring Gardens, which stood in what is now the Precinct's paved square, was demolished in 1959/60. Damp, rat infested and wholly unsuitable for modern day living, they were rightly condemned. Many former residents were moved out to new housing in Sunset Close, off Lichfield Street. Guy's almshouses are seen to the right, while the shop with the blind in the distance is Claridge's butchers.

Below: A modern view taken from the same spot as left.

Left: The eastern side of Lower Gungate (opposite the former Arts Centre) seen here in the 1930s. This is the only known photographic record of houses that stood on the spot now occupied by Garfield Snow and the Carphone Warehouse.

Below: The same view today. The shops are splendid, but whoever hit upon the Precinct as a suitable address must have had Tamworth confused with a down-town district of Chicago or New York. What other excuse could there be?

Above: A view from the 1990s looking from Lower Gungate towards Colehill.

Left: Built at a cost of £62,000, Tamworth Post Office was officially opened on 7 July 1958. The foundations had been laid in 1939, but work was shelved during World War Two and not resumed until 1956. This building replaced the former Post Office in George Street.

Below: When the Post Office relocated into Tamworth Co-operative Society's Church Street department store in 1995, the ground floor of the old Post Office was converted into a Yates's Wine Lodge.

Above: The Post Office site had formerly been occupied by a three-storey Georgian town house, pictured here in 1933 when it was serving as a social club for working men.

COLEHILL

Above: E.B. Hamel's 1829 illustration shows Colehill in the reign of King George IV. The house standing on the corner with Church Street (right, now the Co-op) was built by the Larkin family in 1805. The half-timbered Tudor building in the centre is occupied by Shoefayre in the picture below.

Above: The same view as above in 1995. Apart from the insertion of shop fronts, buildings on the left appear remarkably unchanged.

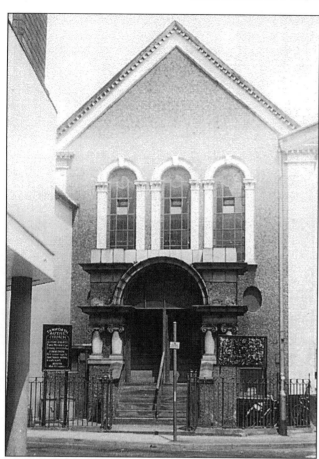

Above: In 1973 a new Baptist church opened in Belgrave and the chapel was converted back to theatre use as Tamworth Arts Centre, opening in 1975. The Arts Centre closed in 2001 and the building was sold by the borough council as a cost-cutting measure. What the future holds for this historic landmark is uncertain.

Above: Built as a theatre in 1709, the well-known 18th-century actor-manager Roger Kemble, along with his celebrated actress daughter Sarah Siddons, performed in this fine Tamworth building which in later years saw use as a pig market and Sir Robert Peel's malthouse before being converted into Tamworth's Baptist tabernacle in 1870.

Right and Below: Tamworth's philanthropic Victorian vicar, Revd William MacGregor, was actively involved in founding the Co-operative movement in Tamworth, buying the Colehill and Church Street corner site in 1884. The Larkin house was demolished and the Co-op's magnificent central premises built in 1896. Adjacent offices and committee rooms were added in 1903. Hideous steel cladding which was wrapped around the building throughout the 1970s and '80s (pictured below) has mercifully been removed to reveal fine decorative Gibbs and Canning terracotta tiles. Colehill was pedestrianised and distinctive new street lighting installed in 2002.

Above: Here we see Gibbs and Canning's float passing along Colehill in the 1933 Tamworth Carnival. The onlookers leaning out from the sash window on the right are in the former Tamworth vicarage, which was to become the Co-op Milk Bar.

Left: The Colehill vicarage, seen here from Bolebridge Street in the 1920s, was home to some of the town's great vicars, including Richard Rawle, Brook Lambert, William MacGregor and Maurice Peel. A building of considerable local significance, it should have been preserved in its original state.

Above: By the 1960s the vicarage had become the Co-op Milk Bar, but was horribly mangled when part of it was 'sliced off' to allow delivery access to the rear of the society's department store.

Left: Pictured here in 1988, insertion of the Milk Bar's large picture window and vestibule doorway had contributed to wrecking what was one of Tamworth's finest Georgian properties.

Above: Back at the carnival, we have a splendid view of buildings on the eastern side of Colehill as they looked in the 1930s. The large building in the centre was occupied by Abbott grocers, dentist W. Walters and the Refuge Assurance Company.

Above: And here we see the same view as above in 1988. Why such incongruous 1960s architecture was deemed an improvement on what went before beggars belief.

BOLEBRIDGE STREET

Above: Tamworth was in the grip of the great snowfall of 1947 when this picture looking down Bolebridge Street was taken. The whole country was covered in a white-over that began on the first day of January – and went on until April!

Above: Recent renovation work revealed some of the ancient timbers beneath the modern plaster.

Above: The Spot was a landmark familiar to generations of Tamworth people. Seen here in 1925, the shop on the corner of Bolebridge Street and George Street dates back to Tudor times, making it one of Tamworth's oldest buildings. Unfortunately, ancient oak beams which are clearly visible in E.B. Hamel's 1829 illustration (page 41) have been covered over with stucco.

Right: Bolebridge Street looking north in April 1964, showing Jim Pemberton's open-fronted fish shop on the left.

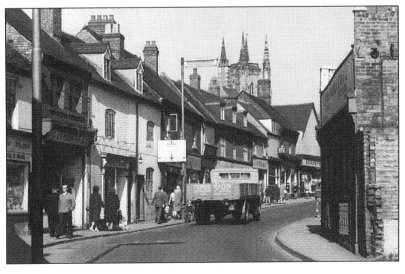

Above: Bolebridge Street viewed from the forecourt of the former Tamworth Working Men's Club in 1970. The large white building was Tom's Café, formerly the Old White Lion pubic house.

Above: A modern view taken from the same spot as above. Pemberton's fish shop is now the Bed Shop.

Above: Max's clothed many a young Tamworth man in the 1960s and '70s.

Above: Pictured here in the early 1970s, only the grand façade of the former Tamworth WMC was retained when the building was reconstructed as J.D. Wetherspoon's Bole Bridge pub in 2001.

Above: Continuing along Bolebridge Street, this view looking back in the direction of the town centre, was captured by Paul Barber on 14 June 1967. Morgan's fish and chip shop was patronised by many Tamworth people of the era.

Above: Originally a Methodist meeting house dating from 1816, Bolebridge Street Chapel became surplus to requirements when the temple opened at Victoria Road in 1877. The building was later used as William Porter's cycle works, then Charles Smith's Auction Rooms (pictured), and finally Woodcock's printing works.

Above: The White Swan Inn… known locally as the Dirty Duck!

Left: This view dates from around 1973, when a county council planing proposal to declare Tamworth town centre a conservation area maintained that, in spite of the neglected state of many properties, the essential character of the market town era of Tamworth's history was contained here. 'Every effort should be made to preserve, restore and maintain this character,' the authority's report stated. 'Although Bolebridge Street contains few listed buildings of high individual merit it has nevertheless retained a wealth of old domestic properties which cluster together along its frontages giving the street a timeless quality evocative of centuries past. If the human scale and historic character of the town is not to be destroyed, it will be necessary to ensure that the essential elements of the area are retained, and that future development is in sympathy and harmony with the historic fabric.'

Above: Bolebridge Street was notorious for its floods and a particularly severe deluge in August 1912 (pictured here) caused so much havoc it was christened 'Black Monday'. Whenever the River Anker burst its banks it was common to see floats, waggonettes, drays, etc., laden with people. Cries of 'all the way to the bridge for a penny' resounded in the street as those possessing suitable transport, and a keen eye for business, turned out to provide a welcome service.

Above: The situation hadn't improved by the 1930s…

Right: …or by the 1950s! Here we see relief coming to stranded Bolebridge Street shop owners in the form of milk, delivered by driver Bill Sheppard in a converted Army truck. In the background is Hamel's tape mill. Today, this area of town has completely vanished, swept away not by torrents of water, but by bulldozers which in 1977 flattened all that we see here to create the Bolebridge 'Egg' road system.

Above: The large square entrance in the foreground led to Queen Street, a courtyard consisting of two narrow rows of houses stretching down to the River Tame. Condemned as slums, they were demolished in 1952. Queen Street was one of several courtyards and small streets leading off from Bolebridge Street. Others included Arched Row, Tenter's Croft and Jones's Yard. By 1974, when this picture was taken, most buildings in the area had fallen into a state of advanced dereliction.

Left: The parlous state of neighbouring properties didn't deter well-known Tamworth cobbler Colin Seal, wearing the white apron, from keeping his shop frontage spotlessly clean.

Above: A last look north before the bulldozers arrive. The building to the right is Hamel's Mill.

Above: Strolling into town in 1978, this couple are passing what was Colin Seal's shoe repair shop. Demolition of the centuries old properties had opened up views never before seen by Tamworth people who were now able to admire the architectural splendour of... the Bolebridge Street flats!

Above: Pictured here in 1979, we can just see Mill Lane, right, which passed through the factory buildings of E.B. Hamel and Son Ltd. The son of a refugee who fled to England to escape the French Revolution, Etienne Bruno Hamel founded the tape mill in 1837. An astute businessman who was twice Mayor of the town (in 1847 and 1856), he was also a talented artist who produced the magnificent 1829 Illustrations of Tamworth. Succeeding generations of Hamels continued the family involvement in both the local tape weaving industry and public service up until the mill passed out of family ownership in 1980, after which it was soon demolished. Today the Tamworth Job Centre and Saxon Mill housing development stand on the site.

E.B. Hamel (1796–1865)

Above: The sliced-off building in the centre it the last of a row of mediaeval half-timbered cottages that had been demolished earlier. During the 1940s, tap dancing was taught by Enid Thompson in the tiny cottage to the left. The chimney stacks belonged to the Red Lion Inn.

Above: Tamworth's first Birmingham 'overspill' residents arrived in 1959, to be accommodated in 'barrack block' council flats standing alongside the River Anker. Although functional, and with panoramic views of the Castle Grounds, they were labelled Colditz by local people and lasted barely 25 years before the demolition men were recalled.

Above: The view today taken from the same spot as above showing the present UCI cinema.

Right: Unlike previous visits, demolition gangs were widely applauded when the flats were flattened in April 1984. The gas holder in the background was erected by the West Midland Gas Board in 1955. The Tamworth gasworks were established off Bolebridge Street in 1835 with Sir Robert Peel as the largest subscriber.

Below: Construction of Tamworth's 10-screen cinema in September 1990. The only regret is that the development faces away from the town centre.

Left: Standing opposite the Knob, this 1960s view shows the entrance to Arched Row, left, 12 terraced cottages built behind the Red Lion Inn and leading down to the River Anker.

Above: Deemed unfit for human habitation, Arched Row was demolished in June 1953.

Above: A similar view from 1974 showing the fabulously named Jolly Button Turner Inn on the extreme right. The 18th-century pub closed in the 1950s and remained boarded up until 1978 when these properties were all relegated to history by the bulldozer. The shop next door to the pub was for many years Thompson's pork butchers.

Left: Originally owned by Lord Weymouth, the Old Red Lion inn was later acquired by the Peel family. In the 1884 Peel sale, it was bought, together with the attached cottage, for the then considerable sum of £1,260 by brewers James Eadie. Commonly known as 'the bottom house'. (See page 50 for side view)

Above: Back to the floods of 1912, we see here the west side, southern end of Bolebridge Street. The tallest building 'Bolebridge House' stood at the northern end of the old mediaeval bridge. Two out of the range of dormer windowed cottages retain their ancient half-timbered façade. By the 1930s, they too had been stuccoed over, disguising their early origins.

Above: The Knob was a triangular area which formed the eastern side of Bolebridge Street. To the right we can see Bole Bridge Garage which opened in 1939.

Above: The timber-framed cottages, dating from late mediaeval times, were demolished in the 1950s.

Above: The Knob, pictured here in the 1950s from the opposite side shown above, was the site of Tamworth's ancient tannery yard. In later years the area was used for parking outside Hamel's Mill main gate.

Above: Viewed from Bole Bridge Garage forecourt, most of the centuries-old street has been replaced by the Bolebridge 'Egg'.

Right: Builders of the Birmingham and Derby Junction Railway solved the problem of crossing the Anker valley by constructing a massive viaduct, consisting of 19 arches, each 30ft wide – apart from one noted skew arch spanning the Glascote Road. One of Tamworth's most recognisable landmarks, the viaduct was officially opened on 4 August 1839, by railway pioneer George Stephenson, of Rocket fame, who drove across another of his engines, aptly named Tamworth, pulling six carriages containing directors and local gentry.

Left: Photographed here in the 1860s, the inquisitive young lady dressed in a Victorian frock coat is standing on Tamworth's mediaeval Bole Bridge, a sturdy brick structure with a history stretching back into ancient times. The bridge dated from before 1316, and replaced an ancient wooden structure. A dog-leg narrow crossing of 12 arches, it lasted for almost 600 years until 1877 when a new bridge was built.

Below: The replacement brick and iron bridge (pictured here shortly before World War One) boasted gas lamps and iron railings, but was described at the time as 'unlovely and dangerous'. It was demolished in 1935.

Right: The third steel and concrete Bole Bridge, pictured from the railway viaduct, lasted from 1935–80. Shortly after it opened, a young Bolehall lad, Jim Bird from Manor Road, discovered what turned out to be a bomb beneath the roadway. The IRA were believed to be responsible, although no one was ever charged with the offence. This photograph dates from the 1940s and shows the Castle Pleasure Grounds stretching way off into the distance, with panoramic views of Hints on the horizon.

Above: A group of pedestrians halt at the bridge in August 1979 for a last look at the Castle Pleasure Grounds, large areas of which were about to disappear under a concrete ring-road which, at night, is today illuminated by hundreds of high wattage neon street lamps blazing down upon miles of meandering tarmac. The disappearance of the 'Colditz' flats was not mourned nearly so much as the loss of so much public open space. The town's modern swimming baths are just visible in the distance.

Left: Phase One of Staffordshire County Council's Tamworth town centre ring road takes shape in 1980 The reason for its 'egg' eponym is self evident.

Above: When E.B. Hamel looked back towards the town in 1829, this is what he saw. He noted in a descriptive text which accompanied his illustration: 'Part of the hostile armies crossed this river on the eventful morning of 22 August 1485, on their march to Bosworth Field. It is a deep, narrow, and circuitous stream. The land on its banks is exceedingly fertile, and the scenery which it exhibits, in many instances, beautiful and picturesque.'

Left: If Mr Hamel could stand on the same spot today, this is what he would see.

Above: A view back along the modern roadway which has replaced the close-knit community that thrived in Bolebridge Street for countless generations.

Right: A recent view from the Arches looking across the Glascote Road towards Kettlebrook.

Below: Ford Cortinas, Escorts and Transit vans were in their heyday when the same view was photographed in the mid-1970s. Advertising hoardings which for many years disfigured the arches have now been removed.

Left: A 2002 view looking back at the Arches from Kettlebrook Road.

Below: In the 1970s, the road system was rather less involved.

VICTORIA ROAD

Above: Returning to the town centre, this is how tree-lined Victoria Road looked c.1904–11, with Thomas Heath and Son's shoe shop, left, and Lawson's, later Deeley's, confectionery shop, right.

Left: The same view as above in 2002.

Below: Tamworth's 1933 carnival queen Miss Lilian Surman's procession passes from Victoria Road into Colehill.

Above: Moving along the street towards the railway station, this is how Victoria Road looked in 1908. Both Victoria Road and Albert Road were named in honour of the royal visit of the queen and prince consort who arrived at the station on 15 November 1843. Hundreds turned out to cheer as the royal party were driven along the newly-laid, gas-lit road under triumphal arches and evergreen garlands to Drayton Manor, the magnificent home of Sir Robert Peel.

Right: The same view as above in 2002.

Above: The site of Hickson's Crown Garage, pictured here in 1934, is now a tattoo studio.

Left: With a congregation founded in 1690, the Unitarian new meeting house is the oldest Nonconformist place of worship in the borough, having been built in 1724. Today, the building serves as the headquarters of the Tamworth branch of the Royal Naval Association.

Above: At this point in Victoria Road, immediately opposite the Wesleyan Methodist Temple, the Mayor and Corporation officially welcomed Queen Victoria and Prince Albert on their visit in 1843. The temple, with its dignified façade, was erected in 1877 at a cost of £4,000. It contained seats for 650 worshippers and replaced the chapel in Bolebridge Street.

Right: The same view as above in 2002. Following amalgamation of the Methodist churches, the temple was sold in 1974 and transformed into squash courts. It was later converted into the Victoria Mews residential apartments of today.

Above: School rooms were added to the temple in 1898.

Above: The school rooms, pictured left, were demolished in the 1970s. A modern fitness centre now stands on the spot in Mill Lane.

Above: Over the years, seven Mayors of Tamworth have had their premises in this pleasant road...Sculthorpe, Bartle, Dormer, Weale, Whitehead, Colbourne and Watson. Pictured here around 1900, we see the road in its heyday, with Marmion Street to the left and Heath Street to the right. In the distance is Tamworth's old brick low level station.

Left: The sales yard of the Tamworth Cattle Sales Company Ltd in Victoria Road occupied one-and-a half acres. Seen here in the 1930s, the yard was arranged with pens and sheds, and provided dining and refreshment rooms for people attending the market.

Above: Two of Tamworth's ugliest buildings today stand on the sites of private residences. The ghastly Tamworth telephone exchange (left) arrived on the scene in 1964 and occupies the site of Dr Sculthorpe's former home. He was Mayor of Tamworth in 1894, 1895, 1898 and 1899. The Staffordshire Farmers building (right), shown in the 1960s, is now a snooker hall.

Above: Decorative iron railings which graced most of the residential properties in Victoria Road were taken away for salvage during World War Two. It would be good to see them returned. Smith and Son's mineral water factory, with its canopied frontage, stood opposite Albion Street. The business was later taken over by Thomas and William Cheetham.

Right: Smith and Son's mineral water factory buildings, pictured shortly before World War One, were demolished in the 1970s and housing built on the site.

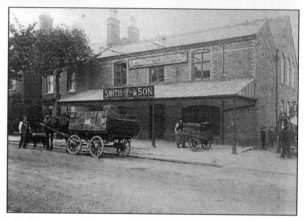

Left: A modern view looking back along Victoria Road.

Below: The same view as it looked c.1926, showing Cartwright's timber yard, left, and the Tweeddale Arms public house, right. The popular hostelry opened in the 1860s and was named after the third Sir Robert Peel's father-in-law, Lord Tweeddale.

TAMWORTH STATION

Above: Pictured here c.1920, Tamworth's much lamented old railway station was built in 1847 to a fabulously exuberant and intricate Tudoresque/Jacobean design. This magnificent gateway to the town was demolished in 1961.

Above: The old station was replaced by a drab, soulless, concrete structure which opened in July 1962. Pictured here in 2002, some effort has been made to improve its stark appearance, such as the addition of a pitched roof, but nothing can hide the fact that this building is simply awful, and offers visitors a bleak first impression of Tamworth.

Left: Established in the 1940s to cater for US troops passing through Tamworth station en route to Whittington Barracks, the Station Café became a popular haunt among young motorcyclists in the 1950s and '60s. It was demolished in the 1970s.

An aerial view of Tamworth station in 1928. The 'high level' Birmingham and Derby Junction Railway (later the Midland Railway) arrived in 1839 and was followed by the 'low level' Trent Valley Line (later LNWR) in 1847. (Simmons Aerofilms Ltd)

Key:
1: Allotments.
2: Nuneaton and south (WCML).
3: To Kingsbury and south (Midland).
4: To Lichfield and north (WCML).
5: To Burton and north (Midland).
6: Low level goods shed.
7: Turntable (disused).
8: Water tank.
9: High level station.
10: Low level station.
11: Lichfield-Burton link.

Right: The opening of the Trent Valley line and station on 4 December 1847. Built largely at the instigation of Sir Robert Peel, the railway company went to great lengths to provide a station that would architecturally befit the town of the great statesman. Designed by Mr Livock, the superb building was 135ft long, the original platform being 300ft long. Clearly defined here are Livock's tall decorated chimneys, serrated roof ridge tiles, high quality specially shaped roof tiles, pointed finials and fretted balustrades. Getting up steam is a Bury 2-2-0 locomotive. Demolition of the old station was an architectural disaster for Tamworth.

Above: Tamworth low level in the 1950s, with an Ivatt 2-6-0 steam locomotive on a freight train taking the slow line through the old station.

Left: The same view in 2002, with a Class 87 electric locomotive on the main line pulling a passenger train from London Euston for the north. The warm bricks have gone, replaced by dreary concrete. There can be few bleaker places to while away time that at Tamworth's cheerless modern railway station.

Right: HRH the Duke of York, later King George VI, passed through Tamworth station on Thursday 29 May 1924. The royal visitor was greeted by the Mayor of Tamworth, Councillor H.C. Goostry, and town clerk Robert Briggs, wearing his wig and robes of office. The Duke came to Tamworth to open the Hall of Memory and extension at the General Hospital to commemorate the 608 officers and men of the town and district who gave their lives in World War One. For many of these young soldiers, Tamworth station was the last view of their home town before heading off to the fields of Flanders… never to return.

Left: Five well-groomed dray horses lined up in the LMS goods yard. There was a time when 38 horses were in use at Tamworth, and for over 90 years, horse-drawn railway drays and vans had been a familiar sight rumbling through the town's narrow streets. The link with the past ended in October 1953, when the last dray horses to work for British Railways at Tamworth were retired, to be superseded by mechanised transport.

Above: Royal Scot Class 4-6-0 locomotive No. 46100 Royal Scot on a passenger train travelling through Tamworth low level station in the 1950s.

Above: Tamworth low level on 30 July 1957 with Royal Scot Class locomotive 46111 on the Comet Express service from London to Manchester, rushing through on the down main line.

Left: The same view in 2002 with a Class 87 electric locomotive about to stop at Platform One with a train from London. The first electric locomotives arrived at Tamworth station in January 1964 to test the overhead lines which had recently become live. Steam was officially eliminated from British Rail in 1968.

Above: From December 1916 until 1919, the Tamworth Ladies' Working League manned a buffet on the LNER low-level platform for the refreshment of soldiers on leave from World War One.

Above: A diesel multiple-unit on a local train to Nuneaton stands at the platform as workmen set about demolishing the old station in 1961.

Above: Tamworth high level in the 1940s with a Stanier 8F steam locomotive on a freight train heading towards Birmingham on the Derby-Birmingham main line.

Left: The same view today with an Inter City 125 HST diesel set speeding through the station on its way to Birmingham. Missing from the above photograph are the signal box, signals, telegraph poles, the old station buildings and two lines to the left. The platform has been much extended.

Below: The station forecourt in the 1930s, packed with carnival revellers.

ALBERT ROAD

Above: A 1983 view from station property showing construction of a new junction at Albert Road/Victoria Road with what was subsequently named Offa Drive leading off to the right.

Above: Dr McColl, who came to Tamworth in 1911, with his children outside his house and surgery, The Laurels in Albert Road, c.1920–1.

Above: The old family home and surgery – minus its railings and with two bay windows inserted – is today the Laurel House doctor's surgery.

Above: Albert Road in the 1970s, with the Albert Hotel seen to the right.

Above: Traditional Victorian housing stood at the junction of Albert Road, left, and Marmion Street in the early 1960s. The corner shop on the right is today occupied by pharmacist Warwick Deane.

Right: When Paul Barber visited the scene on 13 March 1968, however, the view was being radically altered.

Below: Seen from the same spot as above, the area today is a pay-and-display car park. The provision of parking spaces had long been a problem in Tamworth, but sacrificing these houses was a great mistake. Without a thriving residential population, a town centre has no soul – and residents require homes!

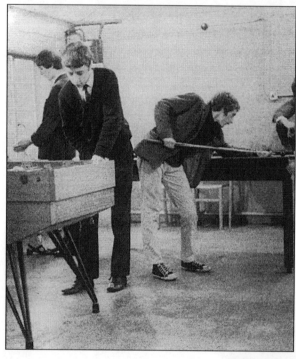

Above: Throughout the 1950s and '60s, these modest premises in Albert Road served as Tamworth Youth Club. The larger of the two prefabricated huts had a hall equipped with a stage and dressing rooms, a lounge and a canteen. The adjoining hut housed an office, craft room and utility room. Paul Barber was a youth club member and took this photograph on 5 July 1967. At that time the club had a cricket team, football team, rugby team and an arts group. Activities included table tennis, archery, five-a-side football, basketball, rounders, canoeing and darts. A photographic club, chess group and music society also thrived. Live groups often played here, including an up-and-coming band called Earth. On stage were Bill Ward, Geezer Butler, Tony Iommi and singer Ozzy Osbourne. On the night of their appearance they changed their name to Black Sabbath… and went on to become one of the world's top heavy metal rock bands. The youth club stood in the grounds of a fine old house which had at one time been owned by the Watton family, who helped establish Methodism in Tamworth. It was later the home of Tamworth Borough Councillor Tom Kennedy, who was youth leader for many years.

Above: In the 1960s, the games room included facilities for table football and snooker.

Right: The huts' 20-year life-span came to an abrupt end when they were demolished to accommodate a £42,000 purpose-built centre which was erected on the same spot. Now known as tamyouth, the centre was opened in October 1970. Unfortunately, the lovely old house had to go as well.

Above: The old youth club entrance hall, pictured in the 1960s, looking out on to Albert Road.

Above: The concert room, complete with bamboo fittings, sea shells, trawler nets and obligatory 1960s jukebox.

MARMION STREET

Above: This early photograph gives us a rare view of Marmion Street, as seen from Albert Road, c.1878–9. The area of land in the foreground was known as Hilly Field. In Saxon days this had been part of a great earthwork which defended the north-east corner of Offa's Dyke. After running parallel with Albert Road, this great entrenchment and bank turned at a right angle, followed the line of Marmion Street and eventually crossed Bolebridge Street to join the River Anker. To the right we can see the rear of Marmion School, which opened in 1877.

Above: From the same viewpoint today, Victorian houses, including a corner shop currently Warwick Deane's pharmacy, occupies what was Hilly Field.

Left: The Marmion Street house being demolished in 1967 is shown on the extreme left of the top picture.

Right: Built largely at the instigation of Revd William MacGregor, the School of Industry was established on the corner of Marmion Street and Albion Street in 1880 to teach young girls the domestic arts. It later became a clinic and was where World War Two evacuees were first examined before billeting. It was demolished in 1970 and the site converted into a long-stay car park (below).

Above: Looking back along Marmion Street towards Albert Road, this is the view we would have had in 1967. To the left is the rear of the Marmion School cycle shed.

Above: The same view as above in 1990. The three-storey homes on the left, known as Offa Dyke Houses, were built in 1880 and, although much altered and modernised, have thankfully survived. The houses opposite, however, have been replaced by a car park. The Marmion School playground wall and outbuildings have been replaced by the perimeter wall of Tamworth police station.

SPINNING SCHOOL LANE

Above: Marmion School, pictured in March 1968, was built in 1877 to a standard 'E' plan design, the boys occupying the eastern wing, the girls the western and the infants the centre. When the former Hilly Field was leveled and the foundations were being excavated, a leaden wrapping containing 294 Saxon and early Norman coins was unearthed, including 33 which had been coined at the Tamworth Mint. Closed as a school in 1964, the historic Marmion name was transferred to the former Tamworth Girls' High School in Salters Lane. The redundant red brick buildings were used by Tamworth Youth Club up until demolition in December 1970.

Right: From the same spot today the view is dominated the architecturally lamentable Tamworth sub-divisional police station, which was officially opened by HRH the Princess Margaret, Countess of Snowdon, on Wednesday 2 July 1975. The local constabulary had previously occupied much smaller premises in Church Street.

Left: The first sitting in Tamworth's new £87,000 courthouse was on 6 January 1970, although the building wasn't officially opened until 22 December when the Lord Lieutenant of Staffordshire congratulated the County Council on the excellent buildings. Many local people were not quite so enthused. The town's magistrates had previously sat at the Town Hall. Paul Barber took this picture in December 1970, as Marmion School was being demolished to make way for the new police station.

Above: This row of six two-storey town houses stood opposite Guy's almshouses. They were demolished in 1968 (inset). At the top of the street is the rear of the former Griffiths Cycle Works, later occupied by Ford and Rowley. The Spinning School that gave its name to the street was started in the 17th century by Lord Weymouth, a former Tamworth MP, as a means of educating and employing poor children. It may well have stood on this site.

Right: Following demolition of the houses, the site was used as a car park for some years until acquired by Tamworth businessman Arthur Higginson, pictured, whose Embassy bingo club was officially opened by comedian Larry Grayson on 23 May 1978.

CHURCH LANE

Above: Photographed by Paul Barber in July 1967, this ancient thoroughfare curved gently around from Lower Gungate to the town's magnificent Parish Church, right in the midst of the town's most historic quarter.

Above: In a period of planning madness, the tiny cottages were demolished soon after the picture above was taken. Paul revisited the scene on 2 February 1990 to take this picture. The brewery advertisement at the rear of the former Golden Cup pub, now a fish and chip shop, has survived although the cottages have been replaced by the Bell Chambers shop and office development.

Above: The 18th-century homes lining the narrow lane may have been short on modern amenities, but they were loaded with simple charm.

Above: Church Lane, as viewed from the parish church tower in 1967.

Above: A 1960s view looking from the Lower Gungate entrance. The large three-storey building comprised of two houses. A set of gates to the right led to the rear of the Midland Red bus garage.

Above: Delightful cottages were replaced by a crude pay-and-display car park, shown here in 2002.

Above: An extension to the rear of the former Midland Red, now Arriva, bus garage was allowed to intrude into this once quaint corner of Tamworth.

Above: Schoolboy Bill Cooper, whose family lived in the pebble-dashed house on the right, strolls towards his Church Lane home in June 1968. Bill, then aged 13, had been enjoying a game of tennis.

Above: On 10 February 2002, now aged 46, Bill was photographed at the same spot. So many changes… but he's still holding that tennis racket!

Above: Boarded-up properties line the lane as we look past a splendid Georgian bowed window towards the Parish Church in June 1967.

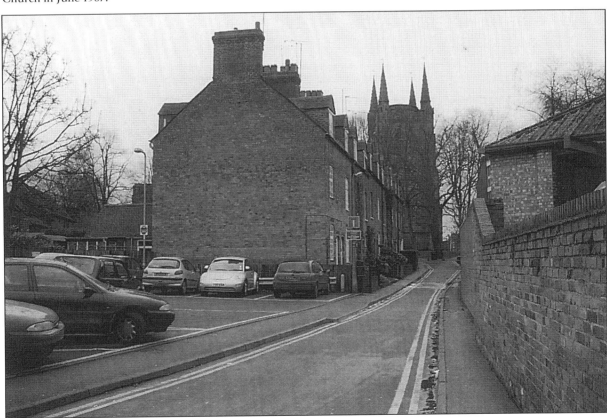

Above: The same view as above in February 2002. Cars have once more replaced homes, except for the fine row of 19th-century town houses that somehow survived the horrors inflicted upon the rest of the lane.

Left: Early 18th-century homes, including Pear Tree cottage at the top of Church Lane, were the main casualties when a large area between the former St Editha's and Aldergate cemeteries was cleared in 1971 to provide a site for Tamworth's new library. Built at a cost of £178,000, the controversial structure replaced the much smaller library in Corporation Street, now the Carnegie Centre. The building was supposedly designed to 'blend in' with the neighbouring parish church and Victorian Assembly Rooms.

Below: The then Secretary of State for Education Mrs Margaret Thatcher planted a tree at the official opening of the new library on 8 June 1973. 'The architecture is magnificent,' enthused the future Prime Minister. 'I'd like to congratulate the architects and contractors on the wonderful way they have designed the library and the trouble that has been taken to see that it fits in with the unique setting.'

Above: Mrs Thatcher's view of the library's architectural merits were not shared by all.

Below: The library stands in the former Aldergate cemetery, the site of which was given to the town by Miss Hester Wolferstan in 1851 when the adjacent parish churchyard became full. When transformed into a garden of rest in 1952, hundreds of grave markers and monuments were uprooted and either used for paving or else simply propped against perimeter walls.

Above: A lone monument marking the Clarson family vault was allowed to remain in its original position.

CORPORATION STREET

Left: Viewed from Corporation Street, here we see Aldergate cemetery, complete with pollarded trees, prior to the graveyard being turned into a garden of rest in 1952. Although well-meant, this act of civic vandalism should never have happened. Gravestones are among the most interesting and informative ways of preserving a town's history, and the records of those who once trod the streets of Tamworth should have been left in situ. Decorative railings which originally surrounded the cemetery were taken away for salvage in World War Two.

Above: Pictured around 1910, the creation of Corporation Street was prompted by Queen Victoria's Golden Jubilee in 1887. The borough council purchased the land in 1888 and 1900 – and determined to lavish civic pride upon the buildings that lined it.

Right: Smith's of Erdington's florist van parked on the corner of Corporation Street in the 1930s. Over the young man's shoulder is a building which has become today's Sir Robert Peel Hotel.

Above: The Assembly Rooms (pictured here during the 1913 Tamworth Millenary celebrations) were erected in 1889 at a cost of £5,500, publicly subscribed, as a memorial of Queen Victoria's Golden Jubilee (1887). The buildings are of red brick, relieved with stone dressings, and contained a public room with gallery capable of seating 650 people, and two ante-rooms and a supper room. Tamworth Free Library, left, a picturesque single-storey building of brick with stone dressings, was erected in 1905 at a cost of £2,000, the gift of Scottish philanthropist Andrew Carnegie.

Above: Pictured here around 1912–14, Tamworth North Staffs Territorial Army Drill Hall, right, was erected in 1911 by the Staffordshire Territorial Force Association. It originally consisted of a large hall for drill, a miniature rifle shooting gallery and an orderly room. On the upper floor were rooms for officers and men. The company who used the hall were 'C' Company, 6th Battalion of the North Staffordshire Regiment. In 1994 the building was given a £435,000 revamp to convert it into a home for voluntary organisations. It is now known as the Philip Dix Centre, honouring a long-serving councillor and former mayor of Tamworth.

Above: Here we see World War One veterans inside the Drill Hall c.1935–6, but it was veterans of the Boer War (1899–1902) who first declared that Tamworth needed a place where part-time army volunteers could meet and train.

Left: Senior members of 'C' Company, 6th Battalion, North Staffordshire Regiment pose outside the Drill Hall's main entrance c.1935–6.

Below: Corporation Street in the 1980s. By this time the former Drill Hall was being used as a sports hall. The former taxi rank on the left of the street is today used as the town's main bus pick-up point.

Above: Tamworth's bus station (pictured in the 1960s) came into full operation on 27 June 1955. The site of Lawrence's former coal yard was cleared, an experimental dense tar road surface was laid to counteract the effects of oil dropped from buses, and concrete bus shelters with glass windows erected – all at a cost of £8,000.

Above: Viewed from Corporation Street in 1983, the following year saw the old bus station redesigned to accommodate taxis that had formerly used a rank running parallel to the Aldergate garden of rest. The buses were turfed out on to the road!

Right: The same view today. A new landscaped snaking taxi rank and a public pay-and-display car park replaced the bus station in 1984.

Above: Many well-known names have appeared on the stage of Tamworth Assembly Rooms over the years, but none more famous than The Beatles. On the night of 1 February 1963, on the brink of their fame, the 'fab four' performed at Sutton Coldfield's Maney Hall (where they are pictured backstage with Gerry Day of support group Gerry and the Phantoms) before speeding to Tamworth where they performed from 11.45pm to 12.15am. The price to see John, Paul, George and Ringo was 6s 6d (33p). Later that same year, 2 December, The Rolling Stones also played a hugely successful show at 'The Assems'.

Above: The Tamworth Herald advert announcing that The Beatles were coming to town.

Right: No photographs of The Beatles in Tamworth are known to exist, but this computer generated image gives an impression of how the group looked on the Assembly Rooms stage during that memorable night. Other 1960s stars such as The Hollies, Swinging Blue Jeans, Eden Kane, The Honeycombs, The Bachelors, The Applejacks, Peter and Gordon, Big Dee Irwin and even Buddy Holly's backing group, The Crickets, played the town's top entertainment venue.

ALDERGATE

Henry Charles Mitchell was the head of the firm of Messrs. H.Y. Mitchell and Sons Ltd, monumental sculptors of 31 Aldergate, with which his father and grandfather had been connected. An outstanding personality in the life of the town, Mitchell combined his business activities (most of Tamworth's old gravestones are the work of his firm) with a widely cultured mind and an authoritative knowledge of local history which found expression through an able pen. Among his principal contributions to authorship are Tamworth Tower and Town; Tamworth Parish Church; A Short History of Tamworth Castle; A Guide and Short History of St Editha's, Tamworth; A Chapter in the History of Tamworth Grammar School; Tamworth Royal Mint and St Editha's Abbey and Parish Church, Polesworth.

Above: The former premises of stonemasons H.Y. Mitchell and Sons, pictured in 1996 when used as a betting shop.

Above: H.C. Mitchell (1873–1947).

Right: The Birmingham and Midland Motor Omnibus Co Ltd opened their Tamworth garage in 1927. But look what they knocked down to build it…

Above: A stately family home with extensive lawns and gardens, The Paddock stood on the site of what was to become the Midland Red, and later Arriva, bus garage. The house was built in 1820 by Dr Shirley Fielding Palmer. His son, Charles Ferrers Palmer, was born here and it was he who, in 1845, published The History of the Town and Castle of Tamworth, the most erudite and meticulously researched work ever written about the town. The Paddock was later acquired by John Lea Jennings (1823–1906), a wholesale grocer and druggist who became mayor of Tamworth in 1858, when he was 36. Following his death in 1906 (aged 83) the Chadwick family took over the house.

Left: The finest grouping of their period in Tamworth, these three Georgian buildings were under threat of demolition when this photograph was taken in 1973. Applying for listed building consent to pull them down, the owners, North Birmingham and District Hospital Management Committee, said they were a hazard to health, infested, in an extremely poor state of repair and would cost a lot of money to restore. But Tamworth Civic Society, formed the same year, had other ideas. 'These buildings could be transformed into attractive houses facing the church and the new Central Library,' they maintained at the time.

Above: Due to Tamworth Civic Society's timely intervention, the decrepit properties shown in the picture above were saved, and in 1979 were given a new lease of life by Fazeley-based property developers R. & M.C. Smith.

Above: In 2000 this imposing 18th-century property opened as Tamworth's new Peel Hotel, named after a popular centuries-old restaurant that formerly stood in Market Street.

Right: This is how today's Peel Hotel looked in the 1960s. The former Horton and Co building was transformed into a hotel by local property developer David Baxter, the same builder responsible for so brilliantly refurbishing the Globe Inn in Lower Gungate. The property had originally been an impressive town residence with two ground floor bay windows and a large central doorway. The inappropriate glazed shop frontage (currently occupied by a pizza parlour) is regrettable. (See page 83 for an earlier view.)

Above: Tamworth Herald journalists and office staff moved from Silver Street to join the company's Aldergate printing works on 15 April 1965. The company's distinctive street frontage, added in 1974, today serves as Christophers restaurant.

Above: The Tamworth Herald moved to Aldergate in 1959 after outgrowing its former printing works in Halford Street. Pictured here in the late 1970s, the company subsequently moved to Ventura Park in 1996. (Top, right): Herald Linotype operators setting the paper at the Aldergate works in 1978.

Above: Tamworth Herald staff photographed outside the Aldergate works entrance on the occasion of the company's centenary in 1968.

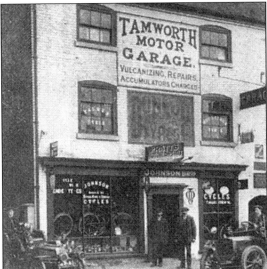

Above: Demolition in progress at the former premises of corn merchants Redfern and Edge on 29 August 1968. The arched doorway led to Hall's Row, a line of 14 three-storey terraced houses.

Left: The white painted Redfern and Edge building had previously been brothers John and George Johnson's garage. The talented engineers began with a cycle making business in College Lane, producing Speed King and Queen cycles, but by 1900 they had branched out into motorbike and car repairs. Pictured here in the early 1900s, George (left), and John are standing in the doorway with their mechanics, who both died in World War One, behind the wheels of two early cars. In the 1930s, the founder of legendary Tamworth car firm Reliant, Tom (Lawrie) Williams, used facilities at the garage to produce prototypes for his three-wheeled vehicles.

Above: In July 1971, the Tamworth branch of the Royal British Legion moved from their previous headquarters in Church Street to new purpose-built premises in Aldergate. Pictured here in 1990, the former motorcycle shop had by then been acquired by the Tamworth Herald to house a new reception, tele-sales, advertising and editorial offices.

Above: The corner of Aldergate and St John Street has changed considerably since this picture was taken in the late 1960s. Among the many delights on offer in Crim Young's joke shop (behind the car) were stink bombs. Perks's later became Trend Decor, before the building was demolished in 1998 and replaced by the present Peel Medical Practice.

Left: A small flat-roofed office of local estate agents Booth and Potter occupied the site in the 1970s before that too fell prey to developers. The present building is currently used as an IT centre.

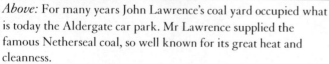

Above: For many years John Lawrence's coal yard occupied what is today the Aldergate car park. Mr Lawrence supplied the famous Netherseal coal, so well known for its great heat and cleanness.

Above, Right: In 1953 the coal yard was cleared and the buildings demolished to make way for the new Aldergate entrance to the town's bus station which was laid out in 1955.

Right: The bus station was closed in 1984 and converted into the present pay-and-display car park. The rear extension to the Philip Dix Centre was built in 1994.

Above: Looking decidedly derelict in this early 1970s photograph, this fine row of three-storey Georgian town houses at the rear of the St John Catholic Church should have been renovated – certainly not demolished. They were unique in Tamworth and, if spared, would today have provided desirable residential accommodation right in the town centre. What price would they have fetched in today's housing market?

Above: Instead of being restored to their former glory, the row was demolished in the early 1970s and the area used as a car park. Removal of these buildings exposed a rather unfortunate side of St John's Church (seen here in 2002), a looming, featureless façade that was never meant to be seen. What a waste.

Right: The St John the Baptist Catholic Church was erected in 1829, since when the steady growth of the congregation has rendered necessary from time to time various extensions. In 1956 the church was completely remodeled and enlarged, with the original stuccoed walls giving way to a most pleasing brick exterior.

Above: The charming building with its quaint bow windows, on the corner of Aldergate and St John Street, had been allowed to fall into a poor state of repair before being demolished in 1968. The Congregational Church opposite, dating from 1827, was originally the Independent Chapel. Prior to the erection of the chapel the congregation assembled in one of the cotton mills in Lady Meadow belonging to Sir Robert Peel.

Above: The same view as above today. A side extension was added to the Congregational church in 1925 to provide accommodation for Sunday school and social activities. In 1974, however, attendance had declined to an all-time low and so the church building was sold and converted into the Victoria Shopping Arcade. It has subsequently been reinvented once more as the Jalali Indian restaurant.

Above: A look along Aldergate, c.1965.

Above: Photographed around 1930, tobacconist and confectioner Mrs Priscilla Reed stands outside the shop she shared with clockmaker Alfred Naylor. The premises are currently Stansfield's hairdressers.

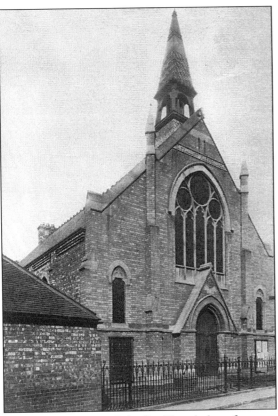

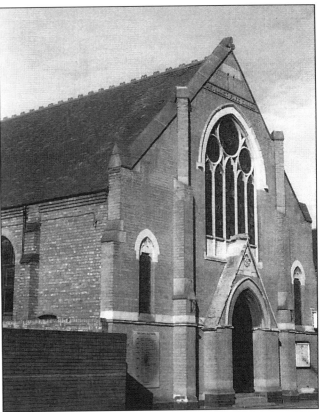

The Aldergate Free Methodist Church dates from 1886 and is a convenient and well-designed building. It was constructed in a striking Gothic style by Tamworth builders T. Watton and Sons, descendants of Samuel and Ann Watton who first received John Wesley's preachers into their Albert Road home in 1771. The great window, with five perpendicular compartments, surmounted by three circular lights, has great dignity. The memorial stones were laid on Easter Monday 1886.

Above: This fine church (seen here in 2002) was deprived of its spire in the 1950s, and the iron railings probably went the way of much of the town's decorative iron work which was taken away for salvage in World War Two. On Tuesday 17 November 1907, the Act of Union merged three separate Methodist denominations into one, known as the United Methodist Church. Several Methodist churches and chapels in and around Tamworth and district have combined over the years, and in 1972 a decision was taken to close the temple in Victoria Road and amalgamate with Aldergate. The building has since been known as the Central Methodist Church.

Above: Standing opposite the Aldergate church, Tamworth Industrial Co-operative Society's wet fish and poultry store is shown here decorated for George V's Silver Jubilee on 7 May 1935. 'Wet' fish, of course, referred simply to fresh fish.

Above: Seen here in 2002, the fish and poultry business has long since disappeared and the premises converted for use as part of the adjacent Co-op warehouse. It is regrettable, however, that a little more imagination was not applied to the task of bricking up the old shop frontage which, for many years, was used as a billboard on which to paste rather shabby advertisements.

SILVER STREET

Above: Had we been standing on the corner of Aldergate and Lichfield Street on 28 February 1968, this is the view we would have of Silver Street. Outside the White Horse Inn the roadway was only 15ft 6in wide, and the footpaths a mere 3ft 5in.

Above: By October of 1968, a massive road-widening scheme had resulted in the disappearance of one side of the street.

Above: The great casualty of the Silver Street road widening project was the White Horse Inn, which still had its iron tethering rings, for customers to tie up their horses, and its stables at the rear. The 266-year-old hostelry was situated on a junction that had become a serious traffic bottleneck along the 53-mile stretch of the main Birmingham-Nottingham trunk road. Time was finally called on 16 May 1968, when licensee Fred Woods and wife Isabella pulled the last pints.

Left: By November of 1968 the old masonry had all but disappeared, and a new presence was looming on the horizon.

Right: The six multi-storey blocks of flats that today dominate the town's skyline were named after prominent local people of the past. Harcourt House, Stanhope House, Townshend House, Peel House, Strode House and Weymouth House are all named after former Tamworth MPs, as was Devereux House, a three-storey block built as part of the same scheme. As Silver Street is no longer open to through traffic, the widened roadway has been reduced to something like its original width.

Above: Pictured here in the 1950s, Felton's garden shop, the Identical fish and chip shop and 'Benny' Davis & Son's famous 'umbrella hospital', where your trusty gamp could be repaired or re-covered, were well-known Tamworth businesses that have long since disappeared from Silver Street. Mr Davis, who was also a hairdresser, caused much local amusement by selling bottles of hair restorative, even though his own head was completely bald.

Above: Smith's tobacco store was adjacent to the White Horse Inn.

Left: The same view as above on 28 February 1968. Two new shops look almost as dilapidated as the older properties on either side. They stood for less than a decade after being slotted into the spot formerly occupied by Davis's umbrella hospital. In the 1890s, the former Identical fish and chip saloon, left, had been a Wine and Spirit Vaults run by Oliver Boonham, who later opened Oliver's hotel in George Street. In 1919 Charles Smith, who also ran auction rooms in Bolebridge Street, bought the premises and converted them into a chip shop. Mr Smith and his wife Henrietta had 14 children, including three sets of twins – hence the 'identical' name he gave to the shop.

Above: In 1968 the Silver Street properties pictured on page 98 were demolished, opening up a never before seen view of Lichfield Street.

Above: Viewed from the same spot as above in 2002, we see that Lichfield Street was next on the demolition agenda. The line of 18th and 19th-century properties running along the street from the White Lion public house have gone, to be replaced by Marmion House, headquarters of Tamworth Borough Council. Originally known as Burlington House and built as a private office complex, this monumental modern landmark arrived on the scene in 1974, hijacking the skyline and dwarfing the neighbouring public house which, amazingly, has survived. The White Lion was built in 1935 on the site of a much older inn of the same name.

Above: Silver Street in 1911, festooned with flags and bunting, streamers, Chinese lanterns and garlands of green leaves and flowers. The occasion is the coronation of King George V. The building on the right at this time housed the original offices of the Tamworth Herald, which was not only responsible for producing the town's weekly newspaper, along with printing tickets, programmes, circulars and posters, but also had an excellent stationery shop which sold everything from drawing pins to office filing equipment. Prior to the acquisition of new print works at Halford Street in 1899, the room above the shop was used for printing

The same view today: Given a picturesque mock-Tudor makeover in 1928, the Herald vacated the building in 1965, moving to Aldergate. The ground floor was for many years occupied by Burdett's shoe shop, and today houses a café and a hair salon.

Above: The Tamworth Herald offices pictured in 1949. The newspaper was established on this site by local businessman Daniel Addison. The paper offered readers 'a carefully digested epitome of domestic and foreign news – with instructive and humorous literary selections.' The big story in the first issue involved a fire destroying many acres of gorse and heather in Sutton Park. The scene, due to the number of spectators, resembled a racecourse and the news that the trees and bushes of this favourite picnic place were ablaze attracted visitors in their thousands.

Above: The very first Tamworth Herald, published on 8 August 1868. The Herald entered the field just as parliamentary election fever was beginning in the town. A letter from Sir Henry Lytten Bulwer, one of three candidates – the others were Sir Robert Peel and Mr John Peel – appeared on the front page.

Above: A rear view of the former Peel Arms steak bar in 1990. The site today is occupied by a Wilkinson's store.

THE HOLLOWAY & LADYBANK

Left: The Castle Hotel in 1851. The Market Street frontage, left, which today serves as the hotel's Bow Street Runner bar, was at this time used as a grocer's shop. But 13 years previously, the hotel had been the scene of a tragedy that shook the town. On the night of 2 November 1838, a disastrous fire swept through the building and claimed the lives of six maidservants who were trapped in their top-storey rooms. The whole town turned out for the funeral when their bodies were interned in the parish churchyard and a great monument erected to record the incident (right). It was as a direct result of this sad affair that the town's first fire brigade was formed.

Above: Seen here in 1908, the Castle Hotel dates from several periods. The oldest section occupies the corner with Market Street, the centre section was next to be built, followed by the ornate gabled block in the distance which was added in 1900.

Left: Standing opposite the Castle Hotel is the Tudor Gothic-style former Tamworth Savings Bank, which dates from 1848. Other splendid properties running along Ladybank appear much today as they did a century ago. The roadway running parallel is known as the Holloway, for obvious reasons.

Above: This 'aerial' view of Tamworth Castle is in fact taken from the Lichfield Street multi-storey flats. It gives us a seldom seen view of the town's most ancient landmark. The sandstone walls are thought to date from the 1180s, having replaced a palisade and wooden tower on the artificial mound (motte) which tradition says was fortified by Ethelfleda in 913. Numerous additions and alterations have been made to the castle by succeeding generations of owners, in particular by the Ferrers and Townshend families.

Above: A group of precariously placed 'penny-farthing' cyclists from Newcastle sail past the Castle Hotel on a wet afternoon in June 1951 as they neared the end of their 250-mile journey to a Festival of Britain cycling rally in Birmingham. The cycles were by then museum pieces and motor car ownership was booming. In the background we can see part of the hotel that was utilised as Ford and Rowley's Castle Garage. A petrol pump is clearly visible on the pavement.

Right: The former garage area now houses the Castle Hotel's night club, which has undergone various name changes since the 1970s including Susanna's, Stripes, Lakins and latterly Minstrals.

Right: Now used as an annex by the Castle Hotel, this fine building at the rear of Ladybank was given to the town in 1750 by Lord Weymouth and Lord Middleton for use as a workhouse. It replaced the town's previous workhouse in Lower Gungate which had become too small to accommodate the growing numbers needing relief. It was once surmounted by a wooden bell-turret (see page 109) and in later years came into the ownership of Edmund Morgan who established his Castle Brewery on the banks of the River Tame, the house becoming his home and brewery offices. In the 1960s and '70s the building was used as the Tamworth 'dole' office, being where unemployment benefit was dispensed.

Left: Along the riverfront side of the building is the home of Tamworth Castle Bowling Club, pictured here in the 1970s. The green was laid out c.1814–21 by Mr John Robins, a London auctioneer who was then living in Tamworth Castle. In 1829 permission was given to build a wall to enclose the ground which has been the scene of many worthy contests over the ensuing years.

Below: In 1930 the bowling club formed a ladies' section, which took over the bowling green on Tuesday and Thursday afternoons – when gentlemen members were not allowed even to watch. But both sexes did come together for Ladies' Day, seen here in the early 1930s.

Above: Established on this site in the 1890s, Morgan's Castle Brewery stood alongside Lord Weymouth's workhouse and the bowling green. It was approached from Brewery Lane, off Lichfield Street. In 1946 the premises were taken over by Britain's largest specialist hinge manufacturers, Gold and Wassall, after they were forced to relocate from Birmingham due to war damage.

Right: Morgan's Brewery employees show off their new chain-driven lorry parked outside the Tame side works around 1920.

Left: In 1968, when this picture was taken, the site was required for new housing. Gold and Wassall, who had used the old Castle Works for 22 years, moved out to new factory premises on the Lichfield Road Industrial Estate.

Above: Modern homes now stand on the site.

Above: Despite its aged appearance, the Holloway Lodge is a comparatively recent addition to the castle. Pictured here around 1910, it dates from 1810 and was built by the 2nd Marquis Townshend as an entrance worthy of the town's great landmark. Previous incumbents of the castle are recalled above its central archway, facing Ladybank, where a stone shield bears the arms of the Marmions. On either side of it, supporting the label mould, are two horseshoes, the badge of the Ferrers family. Another stone shield, bearing the arms of the Townshends, is to be found on the inside of the gateway, facing the grounds.

Left: Near Holloway Lodge stands a statue of Ethelfleda, the famed daughter of King Alfred the Great and widow of Ethelred 'Alderman of Mercia', with her nephew Athelstan. In 913, Ethelfleda fortified the town against the Vikings, who twice raised Tamworth to the ground (in 874 and 943). Athelstan became one of the greatest warriors, administrators and patrons of art to occupy the English throne in the early mediaeval period. Indeed, he was known as Rex Totius Britanniae – King of all Britain! The monument, designed by local stonemason and Tamworth historian H.C. Mitchell, was erected to commemorate the 1,000th anniversary of the fortification of the town by the Lady of the Mercians, and was unveiled by the 11th Earl Ferrers on 9 July 1913.

Left: Tamworth Castle in the 1950s, with the Millenary monument protruding above the perimeter walls of the gatehouse.

LADY BRIDGE

Above: A toll collector receives payment from a mounted traveller in E.B. Hamel's superb lithograph showing the south approach into Tamworth over Lady Bridge. The town's castle and church are prominent landmarks along with the old Castle Mills which were demolished in 1920. The view is from beside what today is the Jolly Sailor public house.

Left: Roadworks in progress at the Jolly Sailor junction of Fazeley Road and Bonehill Road, left, in March 1950.

Below: A modern view of Tamworth from the Jolly Sailor Inn, showing the six multi-storey tower blocks which dominate the town's skyline today. The first block, Harcourt House, was officially opened on 3 May 1968.

Above: A similar view to above from around 1915.

Above: The Castle Mill from an illustration dated 20 February 1841. Nestling in the shadow of the town's ancient fortress, the buildings were actually three corn mills and a fulling mill all under one roof at the confluence of the rivers Anker and Tame. Once owned by the Peel family, various outbuildings were pulled down in 1909. By 1920, however, the mill was deemed 'one of the greatest eyesores of Tamworth' and was demolished, an act which prompted great celebration in the council chamber. In 1924 the site was laid out as a hard tennis court and flower gardens for the then princely sum of £610. The area today is occupied by the castle car park.

Right: The same view in 2002. The Lady Bridge we known today was erected in 1796, and widened at the ends in 1840. It replaced an ancient bridge which had been partly destroyed by ice and floods. Old documents dating back to 1294 name the bridge as 'The Bridge of St Mary', a title it probably obtained from its bearing a pedestal supporting a figure of St Mary or a cross. The pedestal itself has survived and is today placed on the approach to the castle tower. Officially known as the Marmion Stone, it is still used by young children as a wishing seat. After many years of carrying the main Birmingham-Nottingham trunk road into town, the bridge was closed to traffic in 1984.

Above: Tamworth Castle as featured on the front cover of Country Life in 1947.

Above: This evocative view showing the church, castle, Castle Mill and Lady Bridge is the work of J.W.M. Turner, arguably England's greatest landscape painter. The original watercolour was part of a series entitled The Picturesque Views of England and Wales, painted between 1825 and 1838. These were then engraved and published very profitably to the artist. The Tamworth painting, now in a private collection, was executed in 1830-31, when Turner was in his 50s, and engraved in 1832 by Willmore. The impressive building shown on the extreme left is Lord Weymouth's workhouse, which later saw use as Morgan's brewery offices and the unemployment exchange. It is today Brewery House, an annex to the Castle Hotel (see page 104). At this time the building was surmounted by a wooden bell-turret, incorporating a clock and a weather vane, rising from the centre of the roof. This was removed shortly after Turner had immortalised the scene for posterity.

Above: The castle boathouse, viewed from the opposite bank. Originally serving as the Pleasure Grounds' pavilion, this pleasant wooden structure was taken down in 1931 and rebuilt here when a new brick pavilion was built in the grounds. A concrete slip-way and landing stage was also constructed. By 1949 the boathouse was no longer in use and so was fitted out as a base for the town's newly formed Sons of Rest.

THE CASTLE GROUNDS

Above: A 1937 aerial view of Tamworth Castle and Grounds, with Ladybank running along on the top left and the River Anker in the foreground. In 1897, Tamworth Corporation bought the castle at an auction sale in the town, with such of its ancient rights and privileges as had survived, from the Marquis Townshend, for the sum of £3,000, which was provided by public subscription. The acquisition was in commemoration of Queen Victoria's Diamond Jubilee. The castle was formally opened and dedicated to the public on 22 May 1899.

Above: Another 1937 aerial view of Tamworth Castle and grounds with the Castle Bowling Club's green in the bottom left-hand corner.

Above: The Pleasure Grounds as seen from the tower of Tamworth Castle in 1956. At this time the grounds were a hugely popular place to visit, attracting thousands of visitors from all over the Midlands. The concrete bridge over the River Anker, which divides the Castle Grounds from the Pleasure Grounds, was opened in 1931. It replaced an earlier rustic bridge.

Above: The same view in 2002. The Bitterscote lakes were created by the excavation of 340,000 cubic metres of sand and gravel for the new town centre loop road which today slices across the grounds. Strykers Pleasure Bowl opened in 1991.

Above: Seen here in 1937, the Castle Pleasure Grounds were officially opened on 26 September 1931. Creation of Tamworth's 'green oasis' had begun in 1906, however, when enlightened councillors began acquiring strips of land along the River Anker to add to land that had been in public ownership for centuries. The result was a magnificent public amenity of which Tamworth could be rightly proud.

Above: Tamworth swimming baths on the scorching afternoon of 7 August 1988.

Left: When officially opened on 10 May 1937, Tamworth's open air 'lido' was among the finest of its kind in the country. In bright sunshine, members of the Town Council, representatives of other Midland municipalities and a large assembly of townspeople, attended the ceremony, which was performed by Alderman G.H. Jones, chairman of the Public Health Committee, under the chairmanship of the Mayor, Councillor T.H. Sutton, who is seen here making his speech. The Baths covered a two acre site and cost £15,000 to build.

Below: A 1970s view showing the shallow end and children's pool. In addition to a sun-bathing enclosure there was accommodation for 1,000 spectators. Tamworth people flocked here whenever summer lived up to its name.

Above: In 1971, new indoor baths, of a completely modern design, were built adjacent to the north side of the borough's existing open air pool.

Left: The outdoor swimming baths seen here on 16 August 1966. The high-diving board was subsequently removed for safety reasons.

Above: An altogether more depressing scene captured by Paul Barber on 20 November 1993. Construction of the Tamworth Snowdome and associated Peaks Leisure complex sealed the fate of the town's municipal swimming pools.

Above: In 1995 the distinctive Art Deco outdoor pool buildings were renovated and transformed into a children's adventure play area. Not a trace remains of the indoor pool.

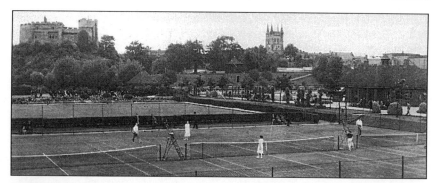

Left: Seen here in the 1950s, tennis has long been a popular recreational activity in the Pleasure Grounds. The six hard courts we see here were laid out in 1931, along with the public bowling green alongside (constructed with lush Cumberland turf) and various ornamental gardens

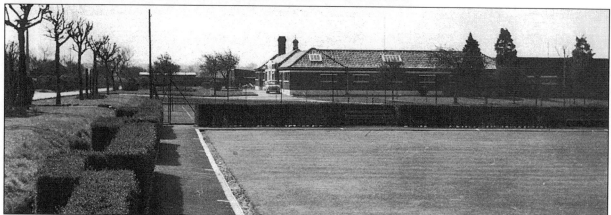

Above: The first match played on the bowling green (seen here in the 1950s) was on 8 August 1932. It was Councillors v The Rest, a team of players from local bowling clubs. The Rest won 67-35.

Above: The same view as above in 2002... but whatever became of the indoor baths built on the site of the tennis courts?

Above: The Borough of Tamworth's new indoor swimming pool was officially opened on Thursday 14 October 1971.

Above: But it lasted less than 25 years before being demolished in September 1994.

Left: Viewed from the Pleasure Grounds, these town centre factory buildings across the River Anker were established as a shoe factory in the 1850s, but were taken over by the Bolehall Mill Co Ltd when it moved out of its original home at Bolehall, near the present Manor Club. Used for the manufacture of tapes and webbing, the mill was extended in 1886, when the 70ft chimney was built, and again during World War One. The company moved to new premises on the Lichfield Road trading estate in 1969, when this photograph was taken. The 120-year-old factory was demolished in February 1972.

Above: The mill had been demolished and the River Anker diverted when the same scene was photographed on 24 February 1978. Construction of the Ankerside shopping centre and multi-storey car park was well advanced.

Above: The view in 2002. Allowing Ankerside's car park such scenic views of the Castle Pleasure Grounds seems rather extravagant, but the development as a whole has contributed much to the commercial survival of the town centre.

Above: This 1960s view from the tower of Tamworth Castle shows how much land the Pleasure Grounds once encompassed. From 1906 up until they were opened 30 years later, household rubbish and material obtained from local colliery slag heaps was used to raise waterlogged sections above the flood plane until the area measured an impressive 60 acres. Crowned with top soil and carefully seeded, the uncluttered grassed expanse was used to stage carnivals, galas, sports events and agricultural shows as well as providing football, rugby, cricket and hockey pitches for local recreational requirements.

Above: This similar view shows the scene in August 1975, soon after the River Anker had been diverted along a new course to provide room for the imminent arrival of Ankerside.

Above: Today the view is dominated by the Riverdrive loop road and Tamworth Snowdome, derogatorily referred to as 'the Cowshed' by local people who have never been overly enthusiastic about the architecture… or lack of it. The complex housed Europe's first indoor real snow ski slope, and only the fourth in the world, when it was officially opened in a blaze of publicity on 9 April 1994.

Left: Seen here in the 1960s, the Castle Grounds' bandstand had been erected in 1900 so that regular band concerts could be given to the public in summer. The embankment was laid out in terraces and flower beds in the late 1940s.

Above: A cricket match underway on the Pleasure Grounds in 1939.

Above: The cricketers had gone by 2002… and so had the skyline!

Above: Tamworth Castle as it looked to E.B. Hamel in 1829.

Above: Paul Barber visited the same spot in 1995 to see how much had changed. The ancient herringbone wall leading up to the great fortress, right, dates from the early Norman period, c.1100, whereas the incongruous erection looming in the background is of a considerably later date.

Above: A modern view showing the Market Street entrance to the Castle Grounds which, up until the 1970s, was approached through a mock mediaeval stone gateway. (See page 128).

MARKET STREET

Above: This end section of Tamworth's Peel Arms pub/restaurant, shown here in the 1970s, was added on to the original King's Arms coaching inn in 1807, replacing what had been Tamworth's first known post office. The enlarged Georgian building was later renamed in honour of Sir Robert Peel, who twice served as Prime Minister and was MP for Tamworth from 1830–50.

Above: This view would have greeted us if we'd popped into the Peel Arms' 'Doubles Bar' in 1987.

Right: In July 1994 the Peel, parts of which dated back to the 1700s, was reduced to just two brick frontages along Market Street and Silver Street, the interior being completely demolished to accommodate the Wilkinson's hardware store that we know today. Although the store has proved hugely popular, and Tamworth is the better for having it here, by voting for the bulldozers Tamworth got it terribly wrong. Market Street was in need of revitalising at the time, but this was short-termism at its worst, a quick fix which wiped away centuries of history – leaving future generations with merely an historic veneer.

Above: The centre section, bearing the 'for sale' notice, was the original Kings Arms coaching inn, reputedly named after King James I. For centuries Tamworth was a border town, with half being situated in Staffordshire and half in Warwickshire. The Warwickshire Town Hall may have previously occupied this site, while the Staffordshire Town Hall stood in Lichfield Street. The hotel premises were acquired by the Berni Catering Company in 1961 and for many years this was one of the town's most popular meeting places. The Peel closed in 1989.

Above: The same view as above as it appears today. At first glance, there isn't much difference – but the façade is all that remains of the old posting house and hostelry where stagecoaches once picked up passengers for London, Liverpool, Birmingham, Nottingham and Sheffield, and the Peels staged many of their great political meetings. The Peel Arms always remained loyal to the family, a staunch Tory stronghold in opposition to the Whigs, who met at the Castle Hotel just across the road. The Wilkinson store opened here in 1995.

Left: Before being pedestrianised in 1989, traffic congestion in Market Street had become a nightmare. Seen here in April 1979, shoppers crossed the road at their peril and were forced to inhale great quantities of carbon monoxide spewing out from endless lines of crawling vehicles. How did we ever live with it?

Above and Below: Alderman F.G. Allton's stores once boasted mouthwatering window displays of cakes, tempting tarts and sugar buns. But shops bearing the former mayor's name had fallen upon hard times when Paul Barber took this picture on 17 February 1968. The buildings were subsequently pulled down and replaced by a modern store and fitness centre (below, left).

Above: Coleman Brothers' Market Street ironmongers shop began trading around 1925, and was a veritable treasure house, selling everything from farm and garden tools, fishing rods and guns to any sized nut, bolt, nail or screw. In the 18th century a brick façade was added to the timber-framed building, which dates from c.1695. Colemans closed on 30 September 1988. It is now a factory shop.

Above: Market Street in all its 1930s glory.

Above: In June 1967 a gaping hole appeared in Market Street. It was the site of a fine 18th-century building which we can see being pulled down five months earlier (inset). The long-established printing firm of Johnson and Allsopp was situated to the left of the building and Timothy Whites and Taylors' chemist and household stores (formerly Lands) to the right. Demolition of these historic properties was bad enough, but the modern Midland Bank (now HSBC) which stands here today is a man-made disaster we could well have done without.

Above: Built in a chateau pavilioned grand bank style, the imposing National Provincial Bank opened in 1837, and is exactly how a bank building should look. Shamefully, it was allowed to be demolished in 1971 to be replaced by the present NatWest building, the awfulness of which is only too apparent.

Above: Former Prime Minister Harold Wilson pictured in Market Street with one of Sir Robert Peel's 'Bobbies' when he came to Tamworth to film a segment for his TV series A Prime Minister on Prime Ministers on 15 June 1977.

Above: Viewed from the Town Hall council chamber, Sir Robert Peel appears singularly unimpressed by Market Street's 20th-century bank buildings, preferring instead to gaze upon 17th, 18th and 19th-century treasures on the opposite side. He is not alone.

Above: E.B. Hamel's 1829 illustration shows the charming old-world buildings that surrounded Thomas Guy's great hall, most of which have been demolished. The Town Hall was originally only a single room supported by 18 massive pillars of stone. The area beneath was used as a Butter Market, where dairy produce was sold. Access to the top room was via a flight of steps at the eastern end.

Above: Tamworth's fine 8ft bronze statue to Prime Minister Sir Robert Peel, sculpted by Matthew Nobel, was unveiled on 23 July 1852. Amazingly, the building in the background sporting the canopy has survived, becoming Goostry's men's outfitters in the 1970s.

Above: Tamworth's famed MP Sir Robert Peel died from injuries received from a fall from his horse in 1850. Exactly 100 years to the day later, 2 July 1950, the town honoured his memory with a memorial service at his statue. The town's incumbent Labour MP Julian Snow can just be seen standing in the same western window of the Town Hall from which Sir Robert reputedly made many speeches.

Above: The Town Hall's crumbling columns and arches were renewed in a six-year restoration project which started in 1968. In the space between the Town Hall and the Peel Statue, the local pillory and stocks formerly stood. The Fine Fare store (now First Choice) arrived in the early 1960s, replacing a building which ran all the way through from Market Street to Church Street. In 1912 this older building had served as the Tamworth roller skating rink, later becoming Fitelson's Bazaar and then, from around 1932 to the late 1950s, Peacock's Arcade.

Above: Pictured here around 1906, the building of Tamworth's magnificent Town Hall was commenced in 1701 and completed in 1702. It was erected and presented to the town by Thomas Guy, a wealthy London bookseller who served as MP for Tamworth from 1695–1708. So incensed was Guy when the 'free and independent' Burgesses of Tamworth failed to re-elect him to Parliament, however, that he threatened to pull down the hall and abolish the almshouses in Lower Gungate, which he had similarly built. Thankfully, neither threat was carried out, although the people of Tamworth were prevented from taking advantage of the almshouses. In later years part of the space within the arcade was enclosed to house the town's Fire Brigade's appliances, which included a steam fire engine. The mansard roof is surmounted by a bell-turret, the bell being rung to summon the Brigade to fires. The clock was presented to the town in 1812 by John Robbins, who at that time owned the Castle.

Above: The fine three-storey property standing opposite the Town Hall (pictured in the 1950s) had formerly been Smith and Garlick's drapery store. They also occupied by the building next door, shown here as Radio and Television Services but now Julie Anne florists. By 1932, grocers George Mason had relocated here from their previous premises at the rear of the Town Hall.

Left: The flat-roofed concrete and glass Nationwide Building Society – a strong contender for Tamworth's worst building – arrived in 1964. Standing opposite the historic Town Hall and 13th-century Castle Gatehouse remains, it is a further example of how modern bank architects have so miserably failed to build in sympathy with the surrounding architecture. Pictured here in 2002, this wholly inappropriate building should be got rid of at the earliest opportunity. If this was to happen, the opened up view of the Castle would be a real boon for Market Street, and the town.

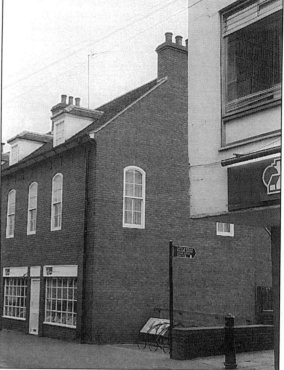

Above: A 1963 view of the Town Hall Vaults public house, which was built directly upon the mediaeval ruins of a late 13th-century gatehouse, part of Tamworth Castle's ancient defences. The pub was demolished in 1974. The neighbouring 18th-century 'listed' Goostry's building followed in 1976.

Above: The same view, pictured left, as it appears today. Goostry's menswear shop was relocated to the opposite side of Market Street and the mediaeval gatehouse beneath the pub excavated to create an interesting entrance to the Castle Grounds. At least some attempt was made to replicate the former building style in the design and construction of the new shops.

Above: This mock mediaeval gateway dated from 1895–7, and was built to create a more imposing entrance to the Castle by its then owner John Robins. Built on top of the 13th-century gatehouse, it was misguidedly taken down when the neighbouring Town Hall Vaults was demolished. The stonework was carefully marked and numbered for reconstruction, 'stored' near the Holloway Lodge – and then forgotten about.

Above: Following meticulous excavation of the gatehouse remains, a new wooden walkway was constructed above the ancient foundations. This has subsequently been replaced by another bridge.

Above: On 20 May 1981 Tamworth Borough Council held their last meeting in the historic Town Hall before moving to Marmion House. Councillor Phil Smith was the newly-elected mayor. The town's future had been mapped out here since the 18th century, although the room was not fitted out as a Council Chamber until 1934.

Left: With the Town Hall to our left, this rare view along Market Street and into George Street dates from around 1906. In the distance is the original Lloyds Bank building, right, with part of John Thornburn's Boot Market, which became the Palace Theatre and later Burton's clothes store, left.

Above: A similar view in the 1920s, by which time Thornburn had converted part of his boot market into the Palace Theatre.

Above: Work on replacing the Town Hall's crumbling arches was still underway when this picture was taken in 1974. The extent of Thomas Guy's Town Hall of 1701 is marked by the construction hoardings and scaffolding. The original single room had soon proved inadequate, however, and in 1721 two rooms were added to the east of the hall. In 1812 these were enlarged, and in 1845 again extended to the east. But how did councillors reach their first floor meeting room prior to the 1721 extension?

Right: The answer could be by a grand staircase similar to this illustration which shows the Old Market House, Poole, in 1761. Points of resemblance between the Poole building and Tamworth Town Hall, built 60 years previously, are remarkable. It is likely that Tamworth Town Hall may have had, at the east end, two flights of stairs leading to a balcony in front of the entrance to the large room.

Left: Here we see Queen Victoria and Prince Albert in their carriage passing the south side of the Town Hall on their way to stay with Prime Minister Sir Robert Peel on 28 November 1843. The contemporary illustration is hardly accurate, but it does give us a flavour of what was a great day for Tamworth.

Above: This fascinating glimpse into a long-gone corner of old Tamworth dates from around 1906 and shows what would later become Peacock's glass-roofed arcade, with the Staffordshire Yeoman and Corn Exchange pubs a little further on.

Above: This front-on view of the Staffordshire Yeoman public house is easily identifiable on the picture, left, due to its ornate and rather oversized lamp. Closed as a pub in 1913, it later became Mrs E. Wheeldon's hardware and toy shop. The Town Hall arches are seen reflected in the windows.

Above: Several of the shops pictured above feature in this atmospheric 1967 view taken from beneath the Town Hall. It is all too apparent that the intervening years had not be kind to these old buildings – but the horror perpetrated upon the former Corn Exchange pub, in the centre, beggars belief!

Above: Tamworth's historic quarter was in a shocking state when Paul Barber photographed this Market Street view of old Middle Entry on 14 June 1967. These centuries-old buildings, which had looked so magnificent in E.B. Hamel's 1829 illustration (see page 124), had suffered appalling neglect and were about to be replaced by a modern shopping centre. If we were to walk through the large opening in the centre (formerly the Corn Exchange pub) we would emerge in the makeshift car park pictured below.

Above: Viewed from the opposite side of Middle Entry's Market Street frontage, the narrow, centuries-old passageway that linked Market Street to Church Street had been demolished and turned into a car park when Paul Barber took this photograph on 6 September 1967.

Below: Pictured here on 9 May 1967, a rare view through what had been the ground floor of the Corn Exchange Inn. The old pub was gutted to create access to a makeshift car park at the rear. The original narrow Middle Entry is just to the right.

Above: The area at the rear of the Town Hall was known as Market Place, or the Pot Market. The shops, so familiar to generations of Tamworth people, had fallen upon hard times – but in better days they were the epitome of old Tamworth.

Above: Kemp's market stall at the rear of the Town Hall in 1922. In the background is the Corn Exchange Inn. Closed as a pub in the 1930s, during World War Two the building was used by the Women's Voluntary Service as a clothes and blanket collection point for bomb damaged families.

Above: When Paul Barber visited the scene on 2 October 1967, he was greeted by piles of rubble where centuries of Tamworth history had once stood. This was indeed the era of out with the old… and in with the new.

Above: From 1968–70, builders toiled to erect the modern Middle Entry shopping development, pictured here in 1992. Whether their labours were worth the effort is a matter of opinion.

Above: One of Tamworth's most fondly remembered businesses, the Clifton Cycle Shop dated from the 18th century and was demolished to make way for the new Middle Entry's main arcade. Pictured here on 9 June 1967, the store opened for business on 7 May 1910 selling everything to keep bicycles roadworthy, such as puncture repair outfits, inner-tubes and replacement gears. The 'To Let' sign was to become a photographic shop occupied by Crowhurst and later Klick photography (below).

Right: Pictured by Paul Barber in December 1967, demolition of the Clifton Cycle Shop opened up previously unseen views of St Editha's Parish Church and the rear of ancient properties in Church Street which were about to suffer the same fate.

Above: Up until 1968, the Town Hall was encircled by a road, enabling traffic to pass right around the building. This was the cause of some congestion and it was suggested in council that the landmark building should be taken down and reconstructed elsewhere in the town – possibly in the Castle Grounds. Thankfully, this crackpot idea was never taken-up. Public lavatories that had been constructed beneath the Town Hall in the 1950s, however, were mercifully removed, but not until the 1990s.

Above: By January 1970, the new Middle Entry development was nearing completion. There were 21 shopping units incorporated in the scheme, the total cost of which was more than £100,000. TV rental company Multi Broadcast was the first to shop to open on 27 February 1970.

Right: Looking at a similar view in 1996, the Market Place area had long been pedestrianised and a raised flower bed added to provide a welcome distraction from the abysmal architecture.

Above: Tamworth has been a market town since ancient times. This view dates from around 1908 and shows Mr J.H. Johnson, in the Panama hat, with his haberdashery stall. The shop behind him, with the large plate glass windows, was at this time F. Buckle's capacious furniture store (pictured below).

Above: Buckle's old premises later provided accommodation for butchers George Mason, before they moved to a new shop opposite the Peel statue, and also the Pearl insurance company. Here we see contractors admiring their handiwork during demolition of the store in 1966.

Left: Today a row of ubiquitous shop units occupy the area behind where Mr Johnson was standing. In the distance, the former Midland Bank (now the Halifax) has replaced Yarrow's clothes shop and the main Ankerside entrance occupies the site of a large 18th-century building, the three dormer windows of which are seen in the top picture.

GEORGE STREET

Above: Seldom can so many poor quality bricks have been laid so badly as in the Middle Entry development, seen here on 9 June 1967. Such woeful design, shoddy workmanship and inferior materials are simply unacceptable for the centre of such an historic town as Tamworth.

Above: The name of the footwear shop in this 1968 view of the unit under construction above admirably describes the architecture.

Above: Early 18th-century buildings on the corner of George Street and Market Street being demolished in 1966.

Above: Shops that line the corner of George Street and Market today.

Above: The windowless Marmion bar, pictured in 1989, replaced the Empire public house, seen on the right of the picture top left. Consisting only of a single large lounge, the pub was officially opened on 8 January 1971, and originally aimed its lunchtime trade at local businessmen 'seeking a hot snack and a quick pint'. Today the pub is known as Mr Qs.

Above: Pre-pedestrianised George Street as it looked from the roof of the Halifax Building Society building on 20 February 1989. Bland, modern architecture has spoiled what was once the most impressive of Tamworth's major streets.

Above: A 1960s view, taken from the rear of the Midland Bank, showing cottages running down to the River Anker. The Castle Pleasure Grounds are just visible in the distance.

Above: A narrow 'L' shaped passageway by the side of the former Midland Bank, seen here in 1971, led down to a group of houses running down to the River Anker.

Above: Established in 1858, James Yarrow's clothes shop was demolished in 1920 and replaced by the Midland Bank, now the Halifax.

Above: With its heavy oak doors, ornamental balustrade, classical-style columns and twin domes, the former Midland Bank was built in 1920 on the site of Yarrow's clothiers and general outfitters. Pictured here in the late 1950s, the building creates an imposing focal point at the top of George Street. Demolition of the Star grocery store, right, is pictured on page 138.

Above: Back in the late 18th century an old Tamworth ale house known as the Angel Inn operated here, although no pictorial evidence survives. In later years the buildings were converted into shops. Many locals remember Whitehead and White's sports and toy shop (beneath the carpets sign) and the Lichfield Laundry which occupied premises next to Lloyds Bank. The shops are seen here in 1975 when they were occupied by Greer and Hughes. This building had suffered considerably over the years, losing two of its three original dormer windows and having the brickwork plastered with white paint, an act of naive vandalism that has defaced many an historic façade. Despite protests from Tamworth's Civic Society, which had been formed in 1973 by local people alarmed at the rate the town's architectural heritage was disappearing, the listed buildings were demolished in 1976 to make way for the main entrance to Ankerside.

Left: Unlike shoddy Middle Entry, Tamworth's immensely superior Ankerside shopping centre has been a huge boon for the town and remains a source of great local pride. Had it not been built, it is difficult to imagine how the town centre retail trade would have survived in competition with the ever-expanding out-of-town shopping development at Ventura Park.

Above: The architectural cost of Tamworth's £8 million Ankerside shopping centre was high. The development not only required demolition of the 18th-century shops to the right of Lloyds Bank, it also signaled the end for the town's Palace Cinema, which had stood to the left of Burton's. Montague Burton's purpose-built tailoring store opened on 3 April 1936, and included a snooker room on the first floor. Lloyds Bank was re-built in 1931 on the site of the company's previous premises. The bank's magnificent brick and terracotta façade was designed to complement surrounding Georgian architecture – much of which, alas, has since disappeared.

Above: Pictured by Tamworth Herald photographer John Walker in April 1976, the gentleman with the tripod is Francis Domaingue, Ankerside's resident engineer. He is standing roughly where the entrance to H. Samuel's jewellery shop is today. The rear of Burton's tailors and Lloyds Bank are in the background.

Above: By September 1979, Ankerside was taking shape and businesses were fitting out their new units. The first shops, Peter Richards Fashions and K Shoes, opened on Friday 15 November. WH Smith opened on 29 November 1979.

Above: Phase two of Ankerside, which extended the concourse through the wall behind Castle Platter, opened in 1992.

Above: Built in two phases, Ankerside was largely constructed around a spacious Sainsbury's store, which opened on 11 December 1979. But the retail giants occupied the premises for only a short period before moving to a new out-of-town superstore at Ventura Park. Their original Ankerside premises (pictured right near the car park doors) are currently occupied by Dunns.

Right: Ankerside has been a great Tamworth success story, and attracted favourable comments from legendary movie actor/director Sir Richard Attenborough when he visited the town on 21 April 1997 to support the election campaign of Tamworth's Labour MP Brian Jenkins.

Above: Ankerside was officially opened by Her Majesty Queen Elizabeth II on Friday 6 June 1980. The royal visit, which lasted about 50 minutes, was the crowing glory for the town which had not seen a visit by a reigning monarch since Queen Victoria… 137 years previously. Tamworth's mayor, Councillor Terry Dix, welcomed Her Majesty on behalf of the town, commenting that it was an event which would 'never be forgotten' in Tamworth.

Above: George Street as it looked in the 1920s. The Empire Vaults public house is clearly visible on the left while the original Palace Cinema, right, its frontage illuminated by fairy lights, stood on the site of what is today Burton's. The first cinema erected in Tamworth, the Palace opened in November 1910 and staged a mixed programme of variety acts and silent movies. The original Lloyds Bank building can be seen extreme right.

Above: By 1960 electric street lighting had replaced gas, but little else had altered. Oliver's Hotel had previously belonged to William Logan, a wine and spirits dealer, and at various times had been known as Logan's Vaults and the Bunch of Grapes. When acquired by Oliver Boonham, who in the 1890s had operated a wine and spirits vaults in Silver Street, the business was renamed after the landlord. The pub retained Boonham's christian name following his death in 1943, and in 1950 was taken over by another popular landlord, Arthur Greatrex, who ran Oliver's up until it closed in January 1964.

Above: As the clock ticked over to 1966, fine old buildings were beginning to bite the dust at an alarming rate. Milo Turner's chemist shop, on the corner with College Lane, was among the first to go. Facey's furniture store, owned by the father of celebrated Tamworth Herald history columnist Mabel Swift, had utilised various premises in the town. For a time William Facey had occupied two shops on College Lane's opposite corner which were purchased by Woolworth's in 1933. The building in the centre, formerly Oliver's Hotel, was acquired by Woolworth's in the mid-1960s and was awaiting demolition in order to accommodate the company's expansion plans.

Above: By 1968, the bulldozers were in top gear as they cosigned more and more centuries-old buildings to history.

Right: The view in 2000. Although the modern pedestrianised street continues to attract fine businesses, buildings that once provided character and uniqueness have been replaced by bland, utilitarian architecture of no interest. Compare this view with the 1920s picture on page 144.

Above: When Paul Barber took this photograph on 18 January 1967, the grandly named Empire Wine and Spirits Vaults was all that remained of this historic quarter of town. The former Empire Theatre came complete with a stage, a remnant of the building's showbusiness past, firstly as the Coffee Pot Inn and later William Tait's Palace of Varieties. In the early years of the 20th century, 'old timers' from the music halls would perform on stage each weekend. All that came to an end as pianist Basil Sigley signed-off on 17 August 1968, and this distinguished Tamworth venue was abandoned to the demolition men.

Above: The Empire's newly refurbished smoke room in 1931.

Above: A greetings card shop stands on the site of the Empire today.

Above: Buildings demolished to make way for the new extended Woolworth's store included, from left, Oliver's Hotel, Whitehead's clothes shop (formerly Kitchingman's), Crutchley's pork butchers and the old Woolworth's store.

Right: Mayor of Tamworth in 1944–5, the splendidly named Richard Milo Turner was a well-known local figure who combined his public life with that of a dispensing chemist. The George Street store that carried his name, on the corner with College Lane, occupied two shops and was acquired by the Boots pharmaceutical chain upon his retirement in the early 1960s.

Above: In 1966 Milo Turner's old shops were demolished and replaced by a modern, flat-roofed building of yellow and blue bricks. The materials and design couldn't have been more unsuitable for a street of predominantly red brick, pitched roof buildings. Boots, who had previously operated from premises opposite, later moved again, relocating to Ankerside in 1979. The aberrant George Street store became Halfords for a while and currently serves as an amusement centre. Woolworth's arrived in Tamworth in the 1930s, taking over a shop on the opposite corner of College Lane previously occupied by Facey's furniture store.

Above: Tamworth's new, much larger, Woolworth store was built in two phases, beginning in July 1968 and opening on 31 October 1969. The fully completed store was officially opened by TV celebrity Hughie Green on Thursday 22 October 1970, when a crowd of 3,000 people pushed and jostled the Opportunity Knocks host to get autographs. The modernised and extended premises, based partially on the site of the old one, was built to bring the store's amenities into line with Tamworth's expanding population. A company sales manager said at the time that the new store had been needed in Tamworth for several years, but they had encountered considerable difficulties getting the additional property required for the larger branch. The dull, monotonous façade that came with it was further diminished when the company changed its corporate shop sign, seen on page 146.

Above: Tamworth's new Palace Cinema opened by John Thornburn on 10 June 1935. It stood next door his old picture house (now Burton's) and occupied the site of his former boot market.

Left: John Thornburn converted part of his boot market to show films. His original Palace Theatre opened in November 1910 and staged a mixed programme of variety acts and silent movies. This photograph dates from 1925.

Below: Many a tear was shed when Tamworth's Palace was torn down in January 1976.

Above: A Wilkinson home and garden store was built on the site of the Palace. The McDonald's fast food chain later took over the premises and spent £300,000 converting them into a restaurant which opened on 30 August 1983.

Above: Thankfully, Paul Barber was commissioned to take a series of photographs recording final images of the Palace Cinema which closed on 1 November 1975. Here we see the main foyer and box office, with a central flight of steps leading to the snack bar, balcony and projection room. Steps descending on either side led to the stalls. The attendance record was variously held by Bridge on the River Kwai (1957), Blue Hawaii (1961), Summer Holiday (1962), Mary Poppins (1965), A Clockwork Orange (1971) and Confessions of a Window Cleaner (1974).

Above: Upon climbing the stairs, we arrive in the café/snack bar. The central doors, left, led on to the balcony.

Above: View from the Palace balcony. The last image to flicker over the magic screen was Walt Disney's Lady and the Tramp.

Above: From its restrained frontage in George Street, the Palace looked deceptively small, but it could accommodate 1,410 people – 954 in the stalls and 456 in the balcony.

Above: For cinemagoers in the 1960s and '70s, interval music prior to Pearl and Dean advertising and 'forthcoming attraction' trailers invariably came from one of two LPs. For most of the year The Shadows could be heard plucking their greatest hits Apache, Man of Mystery, Dance On etc. And during the festive season audiences would be treated to Jim Reeves's Twelve Songs of Christmas.

Above: On 2 September 1939, the Palace Cinema's Tamworth Herald advert informed readers that George Formby was starring in Trouble Brewing. The following day Britain declared war on Germany… and so began World War Two!

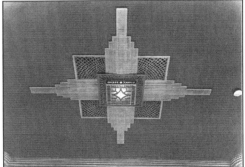

Left: The auditorium's central light typified the cinema's Art Deco design.

Below: The projection room from where Bogart and Bacall smouldered, Abbott and Costello fell about and John Wayne shot countless Indians.

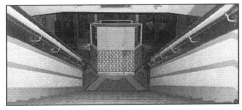

Above: Rear of the Palace's box-office, as seen from the top of the stairs.

Above: Demolition of 18th-century shops adjacent to the Palace Cinema photographed by Paul Barber in 1968. Standing opposite Woolworth's, the property in the foreground (on the corner with Common Lane) was Boots chemists. Shelton's bakers were next door with the Maypole dairy shop on the end.

Left and Above: A few months on and the shops were replaced by a singularly unattractive structure originally occupied by Taylor's cake shop and the Birmingham Incorporated Building Society.

Above: Seen here in 2002, the protruding first floor of tiresome brick and concrete hasn't improved with age. It is astonishing that such an ugly building was ever granted planning permission… but Tamworth witnessed many such planning aberrations in the 1960s and '70s.

Above: The former British and Argentine meat company premises at 12 George Street, on the corner with Common Lane, later became Eastman's butchers. On the left of this Victorian row of three businesses we can see the Bricklayers Arms public house, which was about to be deprived of its contemporary neighbours in another piece of planning madness that defies all logic.

Above: The end butcher's shop and Johnsons cleaners were 'sliced off' and a completely incongruous attachment added. The original Bricklayers Arms section has somehow survived, although it now sits uncomfortably sandwiched between two modern buildings. The old pub is today a Ciro Citerrio gents clothes shop. Sadly, what remains of the Gibbs and Canning façade has been plastered with white paint.

Above: Looking back from midway along George Street, this is the view we would have enjoyed around 1904. The wide roadway and imposing buildings lining both sides gave the area a sense of importance. The double fronted Griffin's jewellers shop later moved across the road to premises near the lower Ankerside entrance. At the extreme right foreground are the premises of Thomas Carrick, framer and printer.

Above: A similar view of George Street in the 1940s.

Below: Pictured here around 1912, William Adie's music shop stood where the Scope charity shop is today. It had previously been Griffin's.

Above: George Street today is considerably less interesting than it once was.

Above: Here we see George Street as photographed by John Walker on a snowy day in January 1979. Bambers clothes store in the centre (now Superdrug) was built in 1963 as a Home and Colonial supermarket. The modern store, with its stark brick frontage, was situated on the site of the original Home and Colonial store which had opened in Tamworth in the early 1900s. Before becoming Bambers, the supermarket had been a Lipton's supermarket. Once again, this view all too clearly shows how this grand street has been cruelly stripped of its architectural integrity and unique Tamworth character.

Above: George Street in the mid-1980s. The road was pedestrianised in 1989, one of the few modern innovations that has made a positive contribution to the good of the area.

Above: The shops on the left of this 1960s photograph were Jenks's opticians and then Carricks the printers, bookbinders and publishers. Carricks was one of Tamworth's longest established firms, surviving into the 1990s, and is today still sadly missed. The George and Dragon public house in the centre had been renamed the George Inn since the early 1900s. The pub was extended into the neighbouring Meesons property in the 1970s.

Left: Here we see the George's new, far from inspiring, entrance as it looked in the 1970s.

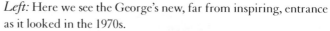

Above: The George frontage as it looked in January 1980.

Above: In the late 1990s, the George received a modern makeover, changing its name to Edwards in the process.

Above: George Street's eastern end pictured around 1910. The attractive light coloured building on the left, with four arched third-storey windows, and a neighbouring building were demolished around 1913 to make way for the town's monumental Grand Theatre.

Left: World War One was nine months old when the Grand Theatre, beautifully constructed of pressed red bricks with terracotta facings, was opened by Tamworth MP Mr F.A. Newdegate on Wednesday 19 May 1915.

Above: The Grand's Tamworth Herald advertisement from 5 May 1945 shows what local cinemagoers were watching on the week leading up to VE Day (8 May).

Above: Tamworth's Grand Theatre was originally owned by Mr C. Dent, but in 1946 it was acquired by the Thornburn family, who also owned the Palace Cinema a little further up the street. The elaborate façade was adorned by a semi-nude Greek goddess which jocular locals often maintained was 'the only virgin in Tamworth!' Modelled by Gibbs and Canning of Glascote, the 7ft 6in terracotta beauty is now on show in Tamworth Castle Museum. Although called a theatre, the Grand was primarily used for showing films, the very last of which was the X-rated Hammer shocker *Dracula*, starring Peter Cushing and Christopher Lee. The building was demolished in 1958.

Above: George Street in the 1940s. The shop occupied by Perks Stores, right, had previously been Chatterton brothers' grocery store which had been established in 1839 and continued trading right up until 1922. The Grand Theatre added enormous architectural authority to the street, which at this time was a popular meeting place for teenagers who paraded up and down the impressive thoroughfare, and into Market Street, on what was at the time referred to as 'the monkey run'. Many young men met their future wives here.

Above: This is George Street in the 1960s. The row of drab shops that replaced the Grand boasted modern residential accommodation above, but they were a poor substitute for what had been one of Tamworth's great landmark buildings.

Above: George Street was in its pre-war prime when this parade of ex-servicemen marched along the road in the early 1930s.

Above: A similar view taken on Saturday 23 July 1932 showing George Street teeming with people for the second Tamworth Carnival, the event having been established the previous year to raise funds for extensions to Tamworth General Hospital.

Above: George Street acquired its name about 1704, its former title being Bullstake or Bullstock Street. This was derived from the bull-ring, which was sited at the junction of George Street, Colehill, Victoria Road and Bolebridge Street. This view, from the spot where mediaeval bull-baiting took place, dates from around 1912.

Above: Tamworth's 1935 carnival queen, Miss Irene Chapman, and her retinue turn from Colehill into George Street. On the right we can see the old Tamworth Post Office which moved to new premises in Colehill in 1958. The former site is now occupied by a travel agency.

CHURCH STREET

Above: Whatever architectural calamities have befallen other Tamworth streets, nothing compares with the destruction wrought in Church Street. Pictured here in the early 1900s, this group of buildings were priceless treasures. The mediaeval half-timbered building in the foreground dated from the 15th century and stood alongside the Tamworth Baths and Institute, a Tudor-style building erected in 1885 by Tamworth's great philanthropist Revd William MacGregor. At the end stand the Co-op's headquarters of 1897, which have survived.

Above: This view from 1970, taken from a similar position to that shown above, shows just how drastically the scene has altered.

Above: The demolition of Revd MacGregor's Church Street baths in December 1966. Part of the old wrought-iron balcony – which was crowded to the limit whenever schools ran swimming contests – can be seen at the top of the picture, while the pool is just visible in the bottom left. The baths had a retractable floor which was covered over for Saturday night dancing. Hollywood film star Mickey Rooney, who was stationed at nearby Whittington Barracks during World War Two, was a frequent visitor here, and no doubt romanced many a local girl whilst dancing over the pool.

Above: Insertion of a large shop front had disfigured MacGregor's fabulous building, the roof tiles of which we can see being removed during demolition in 1966.

Above: The old baths and institute had gone and this area of Church Street was taking on a whole new look when this picture was taken on 8 September 1967. The Co-op's extension houses Tamworth's finest retail store… but the architecture hardly matches up to MacGregor's original buildings. A second floor furnishing sales area was added above the section on the right in 1975.

Above: The Co-op as it looked shortly after this section of Church Street was pedestrianised in April/May 2002.

Above: The Church Street Baths and Institute were a gift from Tamworth's great benefactor, the Revd William MacGregor whose aim was to promote both physical health and self education. The Tudor-style building was erected in 1885 to hold the first public baths in Tamworth. A founding father of the town's Co-operative movement and champion of quality architecture, MacGregor set his architect the task of creating a façade that would harmonise with the mediaeval building (right) which dated from between 1400–50. In 1909 Revd MacGregor presented what had then become known as the St George's Institute to the Tamworth Industrial Co-operative Society Ltd to be used by the members for educational and social purposes.

Above: Revd William MacGregor (1848–1937).

Left: The Institute, with the jettied gable and oriel window, occupied the left side while the swimming baths were to the right. Entrance was through the main door in the centre. Upstairs rooms were occupied by the School of Art.

Above: This superb water colour by E.A. Phipson shows how magnificent Church Street looked at the dawn of the 20th century. Throughout the Middle Ages and up to 1888, the county border had split the town in half with buildings on the right of Church Street, including the Parish Church, in Staffordshire and those on the left in Warwickshire. This curious state of affairs was rectified in 1888 when a census revealed that 2,589 people lived in the Staffordshire half, and only 2,032 in the Warwickshire part. Because it had the greater number of inhabitants, the town was placed completely in Staffordshire. If a similar census was taken today, it would be found that far more people live in what was the Warwickshire side. To the right of Phipson's painting is the 17th-century Stone Cross public house, while buildings stretching away on the left are a rich mixture of architectural styles from mediaeval to Victorian. The half-timbered frontages were comparable with anything in Stratford-upon-Avon, York or Chester. Had they survived, Tamworth would indeed have been able to boast of a street worthy of the town's historical status.

Above: This is how artist E.B. Hamel saw Church Street in 1829.

Above: The same view photographed by Paul Barber in 1995.

Above: The bells of St Editha's Church had been taken down for recasting when churchwarden Mr G. Perry, bell ringer Winnie Chaplin and her father Mr H.W. Chaplin, verger, posed for this photograph in 1931. Mediaeval cusped braces are clearly shown on the first floor of ancient Marshall's Court behind them. The attic and gables were added around the 17th century, making the jettied roof structure a delight to the eye. With the notable exceptions of the Castle and Parish Church, this was probably Tamworth's most historically important building. Nevertheless, it was pulled down in 1932 to make way for the Co-op's new drapery emporium. Only six years earlier (in 1926) Sir Robert Peel's stately home of Drayton Manor had suffered a similar fate. Historic buildings such as these, which today would be recognised as being of national importance, were not then protected by preservation orders, and they were beginning to disappear all over the country.

Above: The same view as above as it looks today. The railings and wrought-iron lamp that had illuminated the church gates dated from 1821, but they were stripped away in another act of lunacy that we shall discuss later.

Right: This rare photograph from around 1930 gives a fascinating glimpse from inside Marshall's Court. Known as Marshall's Yard, this small courtyard was home to a community of six tiny tenements and was typical of many such courtyards that ran off from the town's main roads – particularly in Bolebridge Street and Lichfield Street. We can just catch a glimpse of the church gates through the half-timbered square entrance which led into Church Street. Situated just to the left of the entrance was a tiny store known as the Paregoric Shop.

Above: Moving back through the Marshall's Court entrance into Church Street, this is the view looking back into the courtyard. To the right was a bakehouse and tiny shop where Paregoric – a toffee similar to a throat sweet – was made and sold by a white-haired old lady called Mrs Edwards. The plumbing may have been basic – down pipes emptied rainwater on to the brick lined passage with only a single drain to take the flood water away – and these tiny homes were probably ghastly to live in. But this ancient courtyard was a tangible link with the town's mediaeval past, a past which has been all but obliterated by modern development.

Right: Back in 1936, the Tamworth Herald said it was generally accepted that if the Paregoric Shop could be pulled down, the future was dim for all other historic buildings in the town. A prophetic statement. This was a time when heritage throughout England was beginning to be sacrificed for commercial expediency. Tamworth embraced this irresponsible doctrine with enthusiasm, and only when the era of destruction had reached its peak in the early 1970s were local people galvanised into forming a Civic Society, the aim of which was to preserve what remained of the town's architectural heritage. Sadly, it was too late.

Below: One man who was only too aware of the historic treasure the town was throwing away was Tamworth stonemason and local historian Charles Mitchell who secured possession of the ancient Marshall's Court timbers (each carefully numbered) in the hope that the building could one day be reassembled. Mitchell died in 1947 and his Aldergate yard, together with the centuries-old beams stored there, came into the possession of the local authority. It is generally believed that the timbers ended up on a 5 November bonfire in the Castle grounds.

Above: Pictured here in the 1960s, these familiar Church Street buildings stood opposite Marshall's Court and the Revd MacGregor's Institute. Sandwiched between St Editha's vergery, left, and the Old Stone Cross pub, right, was Mould's Yard a tiny courtyard that backed on to 15th-century ruins of St Editha's Deanery. Access was via a narrow passageway between the three cottages in the centre.

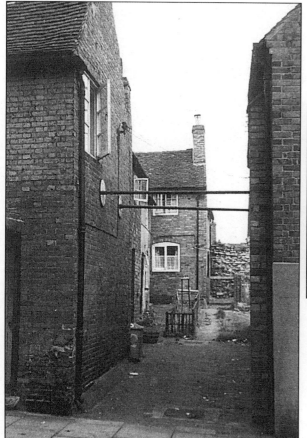

Left: A view into Mould's Yard, with the Deanery ruins in the background. The Deanery was largely destroyed by fire in 1559, although two parallel walls to the east of the church have survived. Several vaulted cellars are believed to exist beneath gardens that now cover the site.

Above: Mould's Yard, together with the cottages fronting on to Church Street, was demolished in July 1969. The old buildings were eventually replaced by a new branch of the Trustee Savings Bank which was officially opened on 7 January 1975. The architects claimed at the time that they had used various features of the surrounding buildings as their framework for the new design which, they said, created a pleasing effect which harmonises with the street scene. Revd MacGregor may have begged to differ.

Above: Among Tamworth's greatest treasures is its Parish Church, pictured here around 1905, one of the largest parish churches in the country. Dedicated to St Editha, a Saxon saint, the church was founded by King Edgar in 963 but rebuilt by the Marmion family following the Norman conquest. On Trinity Monday 23 May 1345, however, much of the building was destroyed in the 'Great Fire of Tamworth'. Over the next 20 years, the church was rebuilt by its then Dean, Baldwin de Witney, who overcame great poverty at home, war abroad and the dreaded Black Death. He died in 1396. The building of the tower at the west end, probably within 50 or 60 years of Dean Witney's death, completed a magnificent scheme.

Above: Mould's Yard, right, was still standing, but other great changes were taking place in Tamworth when photographer John Latham captured this view of Church Street in May 1968.

Left: Wrought-iron railings bordering the Church Street frontage to the parish church were erected in 1821, and were deemed too important to be taken away as salvage in World War Two when practically all of the town's decorative ironwork disappeared. In 1967, a proposal to remove the wall, railings and trees and replace them with a small retaining wall, with a grass slope towards the church, led to a Consistory Court hearing which overruled objections put forward by Parochial Church Council member Mr L.A. Linford.

Right: Mr Linford's historical and environmental concerns that the 'open' grass bank would detract from the dignity of the southern elevation of the church didn't deflect Tamworth's town planners from their chosen path. In May 1968, the railings were sawn down and the church's boundary wall pushed back in order to widen the footpath from 3ft to 8ft.

Left: The project required the removal of memorial stones and human remains (several ancient lead coffins were unearthed), and seven mature trees were felled. Throughout the court hearing, Mr Linford had claimed that there was no reason to widen Church Street at all.

Right: Here we see the end result of all that controversy. The railings, which dated from the time of George IV, were replaced by the present 'open plan' grass slope and the reduced retaining wall was capped with concrete paving slabs. But where's the road… and where's that contentious pavement? St Editha's Square was created in the 1970s, and traffic no longer passes the church. The scheme was completely unneccessary… just as Mr Linford said it was.

Above: Peering over the church railings in 1955, this is the view we would have had of the corner of College Lane. The three-storey property in the centre was Moll Baxter's lodging house, then Williams with 'cheap baths for working men', Huskin's house and then the Waterworks store. They were demolished in March 1956.

Above: Seen here from the top of the church steps, workmen cut the grass along St Editha's southern frontage in the 1930s. The dark-suited gentleman walking away is the Revd Arthur McCreery Coxon, who was Vicar of Tamworth from 1936–49. The buildings in the background (also pictured above) were pulled down to make way for the Co-op's burgeoning central premises (right).

Above: Viewed from the top of the church tower in 1999, the Church Street/College Lane corner is today occupied by the Co-op department store which opened on Saturday 18 June 1960. The top storey was added in 1975.

Above: Popping inside the ground floor of the Co-op's newly opened store in 1960, this is the view we would have had looking across the electrical section towards the College Lane exit. The expanding store has had a massive impact on Tamworth's architectural heritage, but few would argue that the service it provides has benefited the town immensely over many years. Tamworth without its Co-op would be unthinkable.

Above: Upon leaving the Co-op and stepping into College Lane in 1968, this rather dilapidated scene would have greeted us. The whitewashed cottage bearing a sign above a small window was Fretwell's watch and clock maker's workshop. At the far end is the rear of Lesser's furniture store, previously Aspinall's lodging house.

Above: For many Tamworthians, demolition of the five gabled shops that stood opposite the parish church was the greatest crime ever committed in the town centre. Pictured here in 1968, shortly before the bulldozers arrived, these centuries-old buildings were the very heart and soul of old Tamworth. They oozed character and charm and epitomised the ancient market town of MacGregor, Hamel, Peel, and Guy. The decision to pull them down was an appalling blunder which has haunted the town's local authority ever since.

Above: Originally a Georgian residential property standing on the corner with College Lane, this large house was converted into Lesser's furniture store in 1953. The new shop, with its large, plate glass windows, changed the appearance of Church Street considerably – but not quite as much as the bulldozers which were about to consign it to history.

Right: In place of the historic buildings shown above, Tamworth today has a brick-paved square bordered on two sides by the most abysmal commercial architecture imaginable. This is 1960s 'toothpaste' architecture at its worst.

Above: One of the gabled shops dated back to the 1400s and contained a nearly complete mediaeval hall and solar – a rarity which the town, and indeed the nation, should have cherished and certainly not demolished. Another had Tudor windows looking out on to the street. Godfrey's famous boot sign is the only thing to survive from this irreplaceable street scene. It is on display in the Castle Museum.

Above: In the space of 10 days, hundreds of years of Tamworth history was reduced to rubble. Most of the businesses that had operated from the old shops relocated to new premises built at the rear. 1968 was indeed a terrible year for the town's historic buildings.

Above: As Paul Barber climbed the famous double spiral staircase to the top of St Editha's church tower on 14 February 1967, he little realised that he was about to capture one of the most important photographs ever taken of Tamworth. A tree which for many years was a feature of St Editha's Square is clearly visible at the rear of Lesser's shop.

Left: When Paul went back up the tower in March 1999, the view was unrecognisable.

Above: This last look at the Church Street shops shows how they appeared on 28 February 1968. In the foreground, however, the bulldozers had already been to work.

Above: Prior to the arrival of the demolition gangs the gaping hole in the street scene had been occupied a group of old buildings known as Middle Entry and a neighbouring pub known as the Wheatsheaf Inn, drawn here in 1943 by Midlands artist Will A. Green.

Left: Paul Barber's 1967 photograph from St Editha's tower clearly shows where the former Middle Entry and Wheatsheaf Inn buildings had been.

Left: We cannot move on without taking a brief look at the arrival of modern Middle Entry, seen here under construction on 29 February 1968. Such boxy, unimaginative architecture doesn't sit comfortably opposite such a splendid edifice as the town's parish church.

Above: The first phase of new Middle Entry was an £80,000 private enterprise in which new premises were built for existing Church Street businesses, Lesser's, Pauline and Christine Allen's stores, Godfrey's and Matthews' butchers. These new shops boasted a combined frontage of 140ft to Church Street.

Above: The private development was linked to the borough council's £250,000 scheme for 21 shops running the whole length of the Middle Entry from Church Street through to Market Street.

Above: This rather poor quality 1936 newspaper photograph shows the mid-section of old Middle Entry, looking towards Church Street..

Above: The view today, seen from the same standpoint as the lady wearing the dark coat and carrying her shopping, pictured left.

Above: This was how Middle Entry looked after demolition of the centuries-old alleyway and prior to construction of the new development. Pictured on 28 February 1968, the area had become a makeshift car park. The lady carrying her shopping is in roughly the same spot as the shopper in the picture top left.

Above: A young artist sketches the rear view of old Middle Entry in the 1950s.

Above: Continuing our walk along old Middle Entry in the 1930s, we would have arrived at the rear of Frank and Elsie Walton's second-hand shop, right, and the Wheatsheaf Inn, left.

Above: Old Middle Entry and the Wheatsheaf Inn as viewed from a recently cleared site opposite which was to become St Editha's Close. This photograph, taken in 1957, is one of the last images we have of these historic town buildings.

Above: Work on new Middle Entry took two years to complete, and although businesses that began occupying the units were universally welcomed, alarm bells concerning the shoddy architecture had been sounding for some time. Few Tamworthians were impressed by the stark brick walls and gaudy blue tiled entrances. And the arcade's original fibreglass roof proved a disaster which was replaced by a glass roof when the precinct underwent a £250,000 revamp in 1994. TV rental firm Multi Broadcast were the first to open a shop in Middle Entry on Friday 27 February 1970.

Above: Tamworth's 15th-century Middle Entry was an architectural gem that today would be of national importance. A tall jettied building, the upper gable commanded views along the length of Church Street. To the right of the main entrance is the Wheatsheaf public house.

Right: A superb watercolour by E.A. Phipson showing old Middle Entry in May 1903. The era of civic vandalism was gathering unstoppable momentum when this ancient building was sacrificed in the name of progress. What many Tamworth people can never forgive, however, is that having given up such treasures, they were presented with buildings that were clean and functional, but were little more than characterless shells. From having a unique town centre that today would have immense tourist potential, Tamworth was beginning to resemble any other anonymous town.

Above: A modern Barclay's Bank building occupies the site of old Middle Entry.

Above: Had the elderly gentleman relaxing on the bench been sitting in exactly the same place a decade previously, he would be staring out of the bar window of the Wheatsheaf Inn. Photographed by Paul Barber in 1967, the tall archway in the centre led into Hunter's Yard, a private area owned by local butcher William Hunter. To the left of the archway was Carroll's Army and Navy store, and to the right Roy Arnold's barber shop. This had previously been Machin's pickle business. Bob Walters gents' clothes shop, previously Rex Bartle's outfitting store, is today part of Lesser's furniture showroom (see picture above left).

Above and Right: Following demolition of old Middle Entry, a makeshift car park was created. This was used to accommodate Tamworth's weekly market, the last of which was held on the site in 1967.

Below: All remaining traces of old Middle Entry were then bulldozed in preparation for the new Middle Entry shopping development.

Above: Glorious sunshine and hundreds of spectators welcomed Princess Margaret to Tamworth on Wednesday 2 July 1975. The royal visitor was in town to unveil the Parish Church's new west window. Whilst here, the Princess also officially opened the town's new police station in Spinning School Lane..

Above: Princess Margaret was escorted into St Editha's Church by the High Sheriff of Staffordshire Mr Arthur Bryan. St Editha's Close and Church Street were lined with spectators for well over an hour before the Princess's arrival at the church just after 11am.

Above: The smiling Princess, who wore a salmon pink silk dress and jacket with a matching feathered hat, paused at the west door of the town's Parish Church to acknowledge the applause of crowds gathered in and around St Editha's Close.

Above: Pictured shortly before they were demolished in 1957, these 18th-century cottages stood in what was then part of Church Lane (now St Editha's Close) and formed the eastern side of an internal courtyard known as Old School Yard.

Above: On 15 May 1957, Hazel Smith and her father, Fred, made their way past the Old School Yard cottages, right, which faced the main west door of St Editha's Church. The passageway was too narrow to accommodate vehicles, and so wedding parties, and funeral processions, alighted in Church Street and walked past the church's wrought-iron railings. By the time Hazel had returned from her honeymoon, the cottages had been demolished.

Above: This 1950s view shows the great tower of St Editha's Church rising above the rooftops of Old School Yard. The original intention was to cap the tower with a lofty spire, the base of which was constructed and can be seen rising 10ft above the battlements. But owing to a settlement at the south-east corner which fractured one of the nave arches, the building of the great spire was abandoned, and pinnacles were set upon each angle buttress instead.

Above: Job Shipley's tobacco and sweet shop stood on the corner of Church Lane, which at this point was little more than a narrow passageway leading to St Editha's Church and beyond, eventually emerging in Lower Gungate. The building just creeping into the left of this 1930s photograph is today the Colin Grazier Hotel, but was at this time the town's police station. The large entrance led into Old School Yard, which was established by the first Sir Robert Peel, father of the great statesman, in 1820. In 1837 a new school building was erected in Lichfield Street, adjacent to the Boot Inn. This church-like building, which now serves as a bookmakers, made the old school buildings here redundant and they were subsequently used for residential homes.

Above: The same view as above pictured in 2002. Although it was sad to see the Old School Yard buildings go, the opened-up access to the church is a great improvement.

Above: A close-up view of Job Shipley's sweet and tobacco store. Standing in the doorway is the owner's wife Emma Shipley.

Above: Taking a last fond look at old Middle Entry in the 1950s, this group of three people are standing at the entrance to the narrow passageway which emerged right alongside the Wheatsheaf pub.

Above: Here is another 1950s view showing workmen replacing roof tiles above the entrance to Hunter's Yard. The lorry in the foreground is delivering beer to the Royal British Legion club.

Above: Standing opposite Hunter's Yard, the Tamworth branch of the Royal British Legion occupied this building from the 1920s to the 1970s, when they moved to new premises in Aldergate. Prior to its acquisition by the Legion, this was the home of Tamworth Rural District Council.

Above: Pictured here in 1968, the former Tamworth police station boasts a magnificent Georgian façade. In 2001, the building was transformed into the Colin Grazier Hotel, named in honour of the town's World War Two naval hero who gave his life retrieving vital Enigma codes from a sinking German U-boat. A fine monument commemorating Colin and colleagues Tony Fasson and Tommy Brown, and dedicated to all those who have sacrificed their lives for their country, was due to be erected in St Editha's Square in 2002.

Above: Church Street photographed by Paul Barber from the tower of Tamworth Church on 14 February 1967. Tamworth's wartime air-raid siren is clearly visible on top of the former Electricity showrooms' tower... which would undergo rather drastic surgery.

Above: The same view today shows just how much the tower has shrunk, and how multi-storey flats in the distance have grown!

Above: Looking back along Church Street in 1909, the Municipal Hotel, now the Tavern in the Town public house, still occupies the corner with Corporation Street.

Above: The magnificent Art Deco Tamworth and District Electric Supply Company (TADESCO) showroom and office complex was erected in 1936 by Colonel D'Arcy-Chaytor, who owned Pooley Hall Colliery and was the man largely responsible for bringing electricity to Tamworth. During World War Two, the high tower proved an admirable location for the town's air-raid siren which sounded on 138 occasions. There were four occasions when bombs were dropped on the town, the most serious being the night of 16-17 May 1941, when three high explosive devices were dropped on the corporation housing estate at Manor Road, Bolehall. Incredibly, the bombs landed in the road and missed the houses. No one was injured. The longest period of warning lasted 12 hours and three minutes (from 6.23pm to 6.26am), and the shortest lasted two minutes before the 'all clear' was sounded. The siren remained in use as a call-out alarm for local firemen until the early 1970s.

Above: In 1976, an act of crass architectural vandalism was committed when the Electricity Board were allowed to 'slice off' two thirds of the 45ft landmark tower in order to reduce maintenance costs. The clock was re-installed lower down. In 2002 the ground floor showroom area was converted into a Chicago Rock Cafe.

Above: A section of Church Street's south side in 2002. Over recent years the present Oakfields bookmakers premises have served as a carpet showroom and an organ centre and music shop. But many Tamworth people remember it fondly as Wheways toy shop. Sheltons Bakery had been in Tamworth since 1880 when Henry Shelton opened up a steam bakery in Smithy Lane, Wilnecote. During the depression, he hired a group of labourers to build a row of houses in Wilnecote, which later became Shelton Street. Pauline's Pantry is another fine, long-established Tamworth business.

Left: In the 1880s, this high quality town house on the junction where Corporation Street joins Church Street was occupied by the Hamel family, descendents of the great Tamworth artist E.B. Hamel who also established the tape mill in Bolebridge Street. In 1888 it was acquired by the local authority and later put to use as municipal offices. It was vacated by the council in 1980–1, when they moved to Marmion House in Lichfield Street, and is currently occupied by a recruitment agency.

Above: Church Street's northern side pictured in 2002.

Above: These Church Street shops were home to two well-established Tamworth businesses in the 1960s and '70s. Many people will recall buying their first 45rpm single from Green's record shop, and running home to slip the precious vinyl on to a portable Dansette record player or, if they were allowed, their parents' radiogram.

Above: The former Horse and Jockey public house became the Monica Café in the 1950s and remained a popular meeting place throughout the following decade. Following periods as a nightclub and Greek restaurant in the 1980s and '90s, the premises re-opened as Bonds Bar in 2000.

Above: King Street, which connects Church Street with Market Street, had become something of a derelict backwater by the late 1960s. The wall to the right hid the car park and former stables of the Peel Arms Hotel. The boarded-up shop on the extreme left had formerly been Housewives' Choice, a general store which re-located to the newly built Gungate Precinct in 1966.

Right: This same view as above was taken in 2002, and shows how much the street has improved. Businesses such as the splendid Lady Meadow Restaurant, Rage hairstylists and Janic Antiques have breathed new life into this ancient thoroughfare.

Above: Old housing that existed along the west side of the street was condemned as unfit for human habitation in 1952.

Above: Archaeologists dug up the old Peel Arms car park in 1994, but found few artefacts of any significance.

Above: Seen here in the 1950s, the junction of Church Street, Lichfield Street, Silver Street and Aldergate was for centuries known as the Carrefour, a French word introduced by the Normans to signify a place where several roads meet. Stan Stevenson's rather brash 'super snack bar' and Calypso Café was succeeded by the rather more sedate Alice's Tea Parlour, named after Stan's sister. Redfern's butchers shop later become a motorbike centre. Further along was Thompson's fish and chip shop with Nicholls' furniture store on the corner. On the opposite corner with Silver Street is the historic White Horse Inn.

Above: Here we see the same view in the 1960s. Redfern's butchers shop was established in the early decades of the 20th century by well-known local personality Billy Redfern and continued by his son Graham, who retired in the mid-1980s having changed the store to a bakery and cake shop.

Right: This modern view of the same buildings illustrates once again why perfectly good brickwork and stone lintels should never be plastered with paint. Once one does it, everyone else follows... resulting in ruination of the street scene.

Above: Seen here in the 1960s, Tamworth Co-operative Society's imposing supermarket on the Church Street corner with Aldergate had previously been Alfred Sadler's grocers and tea dealer. The Co-op took over the premises on 17 October 1917.

Above: In 1967 the Co-op acquired the 250-year-old building next door, then occupied by Ferneyhough's, right, and Dolly Morgan, left, and immediately applied for planning permission to knock it down. The roof, which boasted three delightful dormer windows, was particularly attractive.

Above: Despite being a Grade II 'listed' building, permission to pull down the old property pictured above was granted, and the demolition men carried out the deed in 1969. The Co-op then proceeded to double the size of their original store with a £70,000 nondescript, flat-roofed, flat-faced brick and glass extension which opened on Tuesday 26 May 1970.

Above: If we had strolled into the old Co-op supermarket in July 1955, this is the scene that would have greeted us... a far cry from today's brightly-lit aisles and sophisticated checkouts.

Above: Staff must have spent many hours stacking cans into those precarious pyramid displays that are just begging to be nudged by mischievous little boys.

Above: Pictured shortly after World War One, the Co-op had acquired its splendid emporium from Alfred Sadler and Co Ltd, grocery and tea merchants from around 1884 until 1917.

Above: The same view in the 1990s. A condition of local authority approval for the 1970 extension was that the whole of the shopfront glazing of the original supermarket would be eliminated. This was on the basis of a complicated formula concerning possible fire hazards and the width of the road outside. Whatever the reason, the result was the ruination of another splendid Tamworth building.

LICHFIELD STREET

Above: Stepping out of the Co-op's Church Street exit on 26 February 1966, this is the view we would have had looking across from Church Street into Lichfield Street.

Above: This 10 February 2002 photograph of the same area shows just how much has changed. The White Lion public house of 1935, right, has survived, but the row of centuries-old property on the south side, including the historic White Horse Inn, has all gone.

Above: Glancing back towards Church Street, ancient properties lining Lichfield Street's south side were the embodiment of old Tamworth, encompassing a close-knit community of courts and alleyways. The square entrance led to Eaton's Yard, six cottages running in an L-shape off the main road. To the left of the entrance was Mounsden's, a beer, wine and spirits merchant, and to the right a book store and wool shop. The arched entrance in the centre led to Mr Faulkner's milk-round yard. This fine building, with its three distinctive dormer windows, dated from the early 1700s, or possibly earlier. By October of 1968 the whole of this row had gone.

Above: Looking from the same spot today, the row of previously hidden three-storey properties lining Silver Street have been opened up to full view. The old Lichfield Street buildings stood in what is now the middle of the road, which has been considerably widened at this point.

Right: Pictured here on 14 June 1967, the former Archer's grocery and vegetable shop (with the blind) is one of Tamworth's oldest buildings, dating from the 15th century. Currently Caroline Jane's bridal wear shop, it's original half-timbered structure is still visible from the rear. The jettied half-timbered façade in the distance (formerly Watson's newsagents), dates from a similar time and today serves as bar one:eleven. The property in the foreground was formerly a Co-op tailoring, and later greengrocery shop.

Above: The large double-fronted property on the corner with Orchard Street is the Queen's Head public house, which closed in April 1967. The launderette next door was for many years Aldridge's fish and vegetable shop. Further on came an off-licence at one time owned by Edmund Morgan, who brewed Tamworth Ales at the Castle Brewery, and later Moseley's. Next door was Polly Grimshaw's sweet shop.

Left and Above: Originally built as office accommodation, eight-storey Burlington House stood largely empty for six years until, in November 1980, Tamworth Borough Council purchased the premises for £1,500,000. On 1 May 1981, the last council department moved into the high-rise block – renamed Marmion House – from the old Municipal Offices in Church Street. Corvettes Wine Bar (above) was a later addition taken over by the council when the business closed.

Right: Decisions on the future of Tamworth today are made in the modern council chamber of Marmion House, quite a change from the days of the old Town Hall. Over recent years, the elected councillors who sit here have, on the whole, treated Tamworth's historic fabric with rather more respect than in the past. But more effort is required in promoting Tamworth's rich heritage, a heritage that should be celebrated and not shunned.

Above: Stepping out of Marmion House, and back in time, this was the view on 26 February 1966. Polly's Pet Shop had previously been Harrison's butcher's, which was taken over by Jim Kingslake shortly after World War One. He continued to run the business under its former name. Once again, however, these old buildings had been allowed to fall into dereliction and were demolished a short time after this photograph was taken. On the extreme right, next to the Boot Inn, we can just see the second Peel school, which was built in 1837 by the second baronet (the Prime Minister) to replace his father's earlier school in Old School Yard, Church Street.

Below: The same view in 2002 is dominated by the Lichfield Street multi-storey flats. The Peel School, built in the church-like Gothic revival style of the 19th century, is now occupied by a turf accountant.

Above: The original Three Tuns Inn, pictured in 1901, was demolished in 1937. It is probable that Tamworth's Staffordshire Town Hall stood on, or very near, this site.

Above: A rear view of the 1937 Three Tuns building from Brewery Lane.

Left: Brewery Lane, pictured from Lichfield Street, wrapped around the left side of the Three Tuns Inn, the front and side of which is just creeping into the right of the picture.

Above: A modern view of the second Three Tuns Inn which was constructed on the original pub's foundations. It was officially opened at 10am on Wednesday 15 December 1937. The first managers were Mr and Mrs J. Tomson.

Right: Seen here in 1965, New Street ran past the Three Tuns pub, left, and down to the rear of the former Morgan's Brewery. Houses standing on the right of the street were demolished soon after this photograph was taken.

Above: Facing towards the town centre, this is how Lichfield Street looked in the early 1930s. The two women are passing Jack Hawkins' barber's shop, which stood on the site of the present Norris Brothers' garage forecourt. At the time of this picture, the garage was owned by Charlie Day.

Right: The same view as above in 2002.

Above: Standing on Norris Brothers' garage forecourt in February 1966, we can just see the Red Lion public house in the distance. This old pub formerly stood alongside the RAF Association's Flarepath Club on the corner with Peel Street.

Above: This 1907 photograph shows the third Peel School, left, built by Sir Robert Peel, the Prime Minister, shortly before his death in 1850 to replace the second Peel School, which had become too small, on the opposite side of the street. By 1907 the distinctive red brick building had been converted into church rooms and is now part of the Shannon's Mill sheltered housing complex. The doorway on the extreme right led into 'Copper Beech', a late Georgian house that in the 1940s was occupied by the Vyse family, market traders who benefited greatly from an extensive fruit orchard at the rear stretching down as far as the River Tame.

Above: The same view as above in 2002.

Left: Tamworth Royal Air Forces' Association had been formed in 1947 by ex-RAF service men and women returning from World War Two. Meetings were held at the Jolly Sailor Inn and later the White Lion pub, on the corner of Lichfield Street and Aldergate, where landlord Jim Pointon hosted the branch for some 28 years. In March 1972, the RAFA successfully tendered for 'Copper Beech', which had been a hotel and restaurant before coming into the ownership of the Borough Council. Although extremely dilapidated, RAFA members put in considerable effort to transform the property into their 'Flarepath Club' headquarters, which opened on 18 April 1974. The Red Lion pub which formerly stood alongside had been demolished in 1967.

Above: Comprised of around 36 homes in two terraced rows, Peel Street ran off from Lichfield Street, past the Red Lion public house, left, and ended at two large wooden gates leading into a paddock that stretched down to the River Tame. These properties were originally part of the large estates of the great textile industrialist Sir Robert Peel, father of the more famous Sir Robert Peel whose statue stands in Market Street. Well over 100 years old, many of these homes were occupied by mining families when they were deemed as 'slum' dwellings in the early 1960s. The paddock was owned by nationally renowned vet Henry William Steele-Bodger, a former president of the British Veterinary Association, whose family still run a veterinary business in Lichfield Street.

Above: The same view as above in 2002. Peel Street, along with Brewery Lane and New Street, was demolished in 1966 to be replaced by the modern development of tower blocks and townhouses we know today. A block of four shops with associated living accommodation was built near the old Peel Street entrance, which is now a car park fronting on to Lichfield Street. The multi-storey flats we see here were part of the first phase of 174 flats of 15 and 16 storeys, garages and three blocks each of 12 maisonettes. Construction was completed in April 1968. Facing us is Townshend House, named after Lord Charles Townshend who represented the borough in Parliament between 1820 and 1835. In the distance is Stanhope House, named after Fernando Stanhope, MP from 1640 to 1660, and behind that Harcourt House, named after the brothers Michael and Robert Harcourt who were Members of Parliament for Tamworth between 1563 and 1571. Three-storey blocks of maisonettes on the same site were named Devereux House, after Edward Devereux, MP for the borough between 1588 and 1592. He was a brother of the second Earl of Essex, favourite of Queen Elizabeth I.

Above: Among the casualties of the Riverside flats development were two houses and a barber's shop occupied by Jack Smith, affectionately referred to as 'Revolver' Jack by his customers. This had formerly been Annie Archer's sweet shop.

Above: The same view as above in 2002. Properties on the end of the row were simply 'sliced off', leaving this unsightly side elevation in the street scene.

Above: A rooftop view of Tamworth's 1977 carnival procession passing along Lichfield Street. The easily identifiable White House, right, was built in 1833 for Mr S.P. Wolferstan and had numerous tenants before becoming the Tamworth Miners' Social Welfare Club in 1927. The club closed in the 1980s and the building was turned into offices.

Above: Looking out over Lichfield Street from Townshend House on 6 June 1983. The gap in the street scene was formerly a Victorian clothing factory owned firstly by Thomas Cook and then, after 1904, by John Shannon and Son. Today, the Shannon's Mill housing complex occupies the site. The building in the right foreground is the RAFA club, seen from the rear.

Above and Left: At first glance, the stuccoed 18th-century property in the foreground and the three-storey Masonic Rooms appear much as they did in 1966. But the modern view (left) shows that the remainder of the row is missing.

Below: The end properties shown above in 1966 were demolished when the Riverside flats were constructed, seen below on 7 April 1967.

Above: The Manor House is one of the best Georgian houses left in Tamworth. This imposing building replaced a much older house where Thomas Guy's mother lived.

Above: The Moat House, a handsome red-brick Elizabethan mansion off Lichfield Street, dates from 1572. When James I stayed at the Castle in 1619 his son, the future Charles I, lodged here as the guest of William Comberford. It is seen here around 1880.

Left: This grand building, as it appears today, has been used a private home, a medical practice, a lunatic asylum, a gentlemen's club and a restaurant.

Right: The ivy clad Moat House, seen here from the rear in 1905, was for a long period the seat of the Comberford family, who supported Charles I in the Civil War. Following the king's execution in 1649, however, they were forced to flee. In 1961, the Moat House was turned into a steak restaurant by Berni Inns, who sold the property in 1990. Left empty and abandoned for some years, the building was eventually put back to use as a restaurant.

Left: In 1936, Tamworth historian H.C. Mitchell noted in his book Tamworth Tower and Town: 'This stately old house, with its low embattled tower, its mullioned windows and clustered chimneys, embowered amidst centuries-old trees, is a priceless heritage from a magnificent age.' So why was the ghastly, flat-roofed extension we have to suffer today allowed to be inserted during the Moat House's time as a Berni restaurant? The fact that such architectural vandalism was ever permitted says much about Tamworth's lamentable planning standards of the 1960s. The unusual 18th-century gazebo in the garden has, fortunately, been unaltered.

Above: This is how E.B. Hamel saw the Moat House in 1829. In 1950 this architectural treasure of a building was offered to the town free of charge by the then owner Dr Lowson. Although the Borough Council eventually accepted the gift, Dr Lowson withdrew the offer upon discovering that only seven out of 24 members of the Council had voted for acceptance. He sold it instead privately to Mr Ashworth. What a wasted opportunity this was.

Above: Today it is difficult to pick out the Moat House from the towering masonry that surrounds it. The multi-storey flats have wrecked all sense of scale and proportion, leaving the stately old mansion an anachronistic relic from an age that favoured elegance and style above simple utilitarianism. Of their era, the Lichfield Street tower blocks are among the best ever designed and built, and residents who occupy the flats would often not chose to live anywhere else. Whether you love them or loathe them, however, they'll remain the most predominant feature of the town's skyline for many years to come.

Above: Pictured by E.A. Phipson in 1903, this range of half-timbered mediaeval cottages stood opposite the Moat House drive. They fairly dripped with all the charm and character of old Tamworth.

Above: The same view as above, photographed by Paul Barber in 2002, is rather less stunning. Wardle Street, left, was created in the 1920s as an entrance to the Leys housing estate which was built on the site of former orchards off Lichfield Street. The large building beyond Red Rose garage is Acacia House (also pictured below), offices of the Tamworth Rural District Council from 1929 to 1965.

Left: A proud motorist shows off his vehicle on the corner of Wardle Street in the 1930s. In the background are some of the old cottages painted by Phipson.

Left: The fine Georgian town house standing on the corner of Wardle Street and Lichfield Street was for many years Miss Shuttleworth's School. It was demolished to make way for the town's fire station.

Above: Tamworth's first Leyland fire engine parked outside the new station which was opened in 1940.

Above: Tamworth Fire Station in 2002, built on the site of Miss Shuttleworth's School.

Above: A view from 2002 showing Lichfield Street's much-extended Tamworth Arms public house.

Above: Due to its location on the perimeter of the town centre, the Tamworth Arms (pictured here in 1977) has for generations been known as 'the bottom house'. It is indeed a suitable place to conclude our past and present trip around Tamworth – for every good tour should end at the pub.

Printed in Great Britain
by Amazon